A PRIMER

ON

RATIONAL EMOTIVE BEHAVIOR THERAPY

Windy Dryden

Raymond DiGiuseppe

Michael Neenan

SECOND EDITION

Research Press
2612 North Mattis Avenue
Champaign, Illinois 61822
(800) 519-2717
www.researchpress.com

Composition by Jeff Helgesen
Cover design by Jack Davis
Printed by Bang Printing

ISBN 0–87822–478–5
Library of Congress Catalog Number 2002111189

CONTENTS

INTRODUCTION

For well over two decades, we have trained numerous mental health practitioners in the basics of rational emotive behavior therapy (REBT). During that time, we have seen the publication of many comprehensive book-length texts on REBT, including some of our own (e.g., Dryden, Neenan, & Yankura, 1999; Ellis & Dryden, 1997; Walen, DiGiuseppe, & Dryden, 1992). Indeed, we have used and recommended these texts in our basic REBT training programs. However, we have often found these texts too lengthy for use in a basic instructional course on REBT and wished that a primer for therapists was available that could provide a concise but systematic guide to the basics of REBT practice. Such a guide was eventually published in 1990. With this second edition of the primer, we have updated certain parts of the text to reflect developments in REBT theory and practice in the last decade.

In Part I, we briefly outline the principles we consider central to an understanding of the practical steps involved in REBT. These practical steps, outlined in Part II, are presented in the order in which we recommend you apply them in clinical work with clients and in your practice in counseling one another.* Part III illustrates the application of the REBT process to a specific case. Finally, an appendix by Albert Ellis, the founder of REBT, provides a discussion of the special features of REBT that help to set it apart from other psychotherapies, especially other cognitive-behavioral approaches.

In the complex world of clinical practice, clients rarely seek help for only one emotional problem. Rather, they more often come to treatment with several seemingly separate but interlocking problems. The brief overview of REBT practice presented in this primer is designed to complement rather than replace the comprehensive texts that can help you deal with such situations and conduct REBT at a more advanced level. We advise that you first read and digest the material in this primer, then consult the resources recommended at the end of this book for more detailed discussion of the therapeutic process. Many other useful materials on REBT can be ordered from the Albert Ellis Institute, 45 East 65th Street, New York, NY 10021-6593. Telephone: (212) 535-0822.

We hope that you will consider this primer to be a helpful introduction to REBT and that you will find REBT to be a valuable approach in helping your clients overcome their emotional and behavioral difficulties.

---

*Peer counseling is used in all the basic training programs of the Albert Ellis Institute and is an excellent way of practicing REBT. We strongly recommend that you consult the step-by-step guidelines in this primer regularly during peer counseling.

Part I

THEORY

In the first part of this primer, we outline some central principles of REBT, first considering the meaning of the terms *rationality* and *irrationality* as they are used in REBT. Next, we discuss REBT's well-known ABC framework and define three basic *musts* that interfere with rational thinking and behavior. We subsequently describe two basic biological human tendencies and two fundamental human disturbances that are relevant to the theory and practice of REBT and briefly outline the REBT theory of change. Finally, we provide a succinct overview of REBT theory.

RATIONALITY VERSUS IRRATIONALITY

In REBT, to be rational, it is necessary to be (a) flexible and non-extreme, (b) pragmatic, (c) logical, and (d) reality based. Thus *rationality* is defined as that which is adaptable and moderate, helps people to achieve their basic goals and purposes, is logical (nonabsolutist), and is empirically consistent with reality. Conversely, *irrationality* refers to that which is rigid and extreme, prevents people from achieving their basic goals and purposes, is illogical (especially, dogmatic and "musturbatory"), and is empirically inconsistent with reality.

THE ABC FRAMEWORK

The ABC framework is the cornerstone of REBT practice. The A in this framework stands for an *activating event*, which may be either external or internal to your client. When A refers to an external event, we can say that it actually occurred if descriptions of it can be confirmed as accurate by neutral observers (i.e., the principle of confirmable reality). Some REBT therapists prefer to include only confirmable events or events imagined by the client under A, grouping all cognitive activity (including inferences) under B. In this primer, however, A will also stand for your client's inferences or interpretations about the activating event.

B stands for *beliefs*. These are evaluative cognitions or constructed views of the world that are either rigid or flexible and extreme or nonextreme. When these beliefs are rigid, they are called *irrational beliefs* and take the form of musts, absolute shoulds, have-tos, got-tos, and so forth. When your clients adhere to rigid premises (e.g., "I must never make any mistakes"), they will also tend to draw irrational conclusions on the basis of them. These irrational conclusions are extreme and take the following forms:

1. Awfulizing: Your clients will express the belief that a situation is more than 100 percent bad, worse than it absolutely should be.

2. Low frustration tolerance: Your clients will say they cannot envision being able to endure situations or have any happiness at all if what they demand must not exist actually exists.

3. Depreciation: Your clients will tend to disparage themselves, others, and/or life conditions.

When your clients' beliefs are flexible, they are called *rational beliefs*. Rational beliefs often take the form of desires, wishes, wants, and preferences. These beliefs are not transformed by your clients into dogmatic musts, shoulds, oughts, and so on. When your clients adhere to such flexible premises, they will tend to draw rational conclusions from them. These non-extreme conclusions take the following forms:

1. Anti-awfulizing: Your clients will conclude, "It's bad, but it's not terrible," rather than "It's awful," when faced with a negative activating event.

2. Higher frustration tolerance: Your clients will express statements of endurance. They may say, for example, "I don't like it, but I can bear it."

3. Acceptance: Your clients will accept themselves and others as fallible human beings who cannot legitimately be given a single global rating. They will also accept the world and life conditions as being complex—composed of good, bad, and neutral elements. Thus they will also refrain from giving the world a global rating.

C in the ABC framework stands for the emotional, behavioral, and cognitive *consequences* of your clients' beliefs about A. The C's that follow from irrational beliefs about negative A's will be disturbed and are called unhealthy negative consequences, whereas the C's that follow from rational beliefs about negative A's will be undisturbed and are termed healthy negative consequences (Ellis, 1994; these unhealthy and healthy negative consequences were previously called inappropriate and appropriate negative consequences, respectively).

One of these consequences involves the emotions associated with an activating event. These emotions are of two types. The first, unhealthy negative emotions, are unhealthy for any one or more of the following reasons:

1. They lead to the experience of a great deal of psychic pain and discomfort.

2. They motivate one to engage in self-defeating behavior.

3. They prevent one from carrying out behavior necessary to reach one's goals.

4. They lead to dysfunctional thinking.

Conversely, the second type of emotions, healthy negative emotions, are healthy for any one or more of the following reasons:

1. They alert one that one's goals are being blocked but do not immobilize one.

2. They motivate one to engage in self-enhancing behavior.

3. They encourage the successful execution of behavior necessary to reach one's goals.

4. They lead to constructive and focused thinking.

Table 1 outlines some of the major emotional problems for which clients seek therapy and lists their healthy alternatives. Included are both the type of belief and the inferences most commonly associated with each of these emotions.

As Table 1 shows, unhealthy negative emotions are underpinned by irrational beliefs, whereas healthy negative emotions are under-pinned by rational beliefs. For example, an anxious person might believe, "I must get that promotion, and my life will be awful if I don't," whereas a feeling of concern occurs if the person believes, "I very much want to get that promotion, but there is no reason why I *must* get what I want. If I don't get it, that would be most unfortu-nate, but certainly not awful."

THREE BASIC MUSTS

Although your clients will express their irrational beliefs in per-sonally distinctive terms, you may find it helpful to consider these individualistic beliefs to be variations of three basic musts. These involve the following types of demands:

1. Demands about self: This must is frequently revealed in state-ments such as "I must do well and be approved by significant others, and if I'm not, then it's awful" or "I can't stand it, and I am a damnable person to some degree when I am not loved or when I do not do well." Beliefs based on this must often lead to anxiety, depression, shame, and guilt.

2. Demands about others: This must is often expressed in state-ments like "You must treat me well and justly, and it's awful and I can't bear it when you don't" or "You are damnable when you don't treat me well, and you deserve to be punished for doing what you must not do." Beliefs based on this must are associ-ated with feelings of damning anger and rage, as well as with passive-aggressiveness and acts of violence.

3. Demands about world/life conditions: This must often takes the form of the belief that "Life conditions under which I live must absolutely be the way I want them to be, and if they are not, it's terrible, I can't stand it, poor me." Such beliefs are associated with feelings of self-pity and hurt, as well as with problems of self-discipline (e.g., procrastination or addictive behavior).

INTERACTION OF A, B, AND C

In our simple presentation of the ABC framework, it is assumed that activating events and/or inferences about these events (A's)

TABLE 1   Unhealthy and Healthy Negative Emotions and Their Cognitive Correlates

Inference Related to Personal Domain	Type of Belief	Emotion	Healthiness of Emotion
Threat or danger	Irrational	Anxiety	Unhealthy
	Rational	Concern	Healthy
Loss (with implications for future); failure	Irrational	Depression	Unhealthy
	Rational	Sadness	Healthy
Breaking of personal rule (other or self); other threatens self; frustration	Irrational	Damning anger	Unhealthy
	Rational	Nondamning anger	Healthy
Breaking of own moral code; failing to live up to own moral code; hurting someone's feelings	Irrational	Guilt	Unhealthy
	Rational	Remorse	Healthy
Other betrays or lets down self (self nondeserving)	Irrational	Hurt	Unhealthy
	Rational	Sorrow	Healthy
Threat to a significant relationship posed by another	Irrational	Morbid jealousy	Unhealthy
	Rational	Nonmorbid jealousy	Healthy
Personal weakness revealed publicly— others' judgment of self negative; personal weakness revealed to self with others' negative judgment of self in mind	Irrational	Shame	Unhealthy
	Rational	Disappointment	Healthy
Other has something of value not possessed by self	Irrational	Envy (spiteful)	Unhealthy
	Rational	Envy (nonspiteful)	Healthy

Note. An *inference* is an interpretation that goes beyond observable reality but gives meaning to it; may be accurate or inaccurate. *Personal domain* refers to those tangible or intangible objects with which a person has an involvement (Beck, 1976). Rational emotive behavioral theory distinguishes between ego and comfort aspects of the personal domain, although these aspects frequently interact.

7

trigger evaluative beliefs (B's), which in turn lead to feelings and behaviors (C's). In reality, A, B, and C frequently interact in quite complex ways (Ellis, 1985). This process is known as *psychological interactionism*.

For example, your clients' dogmatic beliefs at B will often lead them to reach an overly negative inference at A or to focus on particular features of A that they might not attend to if they had more rational beliefs. Thus, if your clients dogmatically believe that they must not be socially rejected, they may overestimate the likelihood of being rejected and focus on the negative statements others make about them, to the exclusion of more neutral or positive statements. In similar fashion, having certain feelings (C's) such as depression may cause clients to evaluate events (B's) in an overly negative way. Furthermore, being in a certain context at A may influence your clients to make certain evaluations (B's) that they might not make if they were in another context. For example, being in a dark, unfamiliar room might evoke more anxiety-creating beliefs than being in a well-lit, familiar room.

Because a full analysis of the ways in which A, B, and C interact is beyond the scope of this discussion, we suggest that you consult the texts listed at the end of this primer for further information.

TWO BASIC BIOLOGICAL TENDENCIES

Albert Ellis has made the important point that people very easily tend to transform their desires into absolute musts, particularly when those desires are strong (Ellis, 1976). The fact that we seem to do this so easily and frequently has led Ellis to conclude that this pattern constitutes a basic biological tendency in most, if not all, humans. Although Ellis does acknowledge that social influences also have an effect in this regard, he has noted that "even if everybody had had the most rational upbringing, virtually all humans would often irrationally transform their individual and social preferences into absolute demands on (a) themselves, (b) other people, and (c) the universe around them" (Ellis, 1984a, p. 20).

As Ellis points out, however, humans have a second basic biological tendency: the power of choice and the ability to identify, challenge, and change irrational thinking. So, although the tendency to think irrationally may in part have a strong biological component, we are not slaves to this tendency. We can strive to overcome it by repeatedly working to change our irrational beliefs.

TWO FUNDAMENTAL HUMAN DISTURBANCES

Ellis has noted that human psychological problems can be loosely divided into two major categories: ego disturbance and discomfort disturbance. Ego disturbance relates to the demands that we place on ourselves and the consequent negative self-ratings that we make when we fail to live up to our self-imposed demands. Furthermore, ego-disturbance issues may underpin what at first glance appear to be demands made of others or of life conditions. Thus your client may be angry with someone who is acting in a way that she perceives as a threat to her "self-esteem." The fact that her anger is directed towards the other person serves the purpose of protecting her own "shaky self-esteem."

Discomfort disturbance, on the other hand, is more closely related to the domain of human comfort and occurs when we make dogmatic commands that comfort and comfortable life conditions must exist. Ego and discomfort disturbance are not discrete categories but can frequently overlap, as when, for example, a client berates himself as weak (ego disturbance) for being unable to cope with a stressful work environment (discomfort disturbance). The rational solution to ego disturbance is to strive for unconditional self-acceptance; for discomfort disturbance, it is to acquire a philosophy of higher frustration tolerance.

THEORY OF CHANGE IN REBT

Given that we are not slaves to our tendency to think irrationally, REBT argues that we can change, particularly if we internalize three major insights:

1. Past or present activating events do not "cause" our disturbed emotional and behavioral consequences. Rather, our disturbed feelings and behaviors are largely created by our rigid and extreme irrational beliefs about these activating events.

2. Irrespective of how we have disturbed ourselves in the past, we remain disturbed chiefly because we keep reindoctrinating ourselves with our irrational beliefs.

3. Because we are human and very easily (and to some degree, naturally) tend to disturb ourselves, and because we find it easy to cling to our self-defeating thoughts, feelings, and actions, we can overcome our disturbances in the long run mainly by working hard and repeatedly questioning our irrational beliefs and the effects of these beliefs.

OVERVIEW OF REBT THEORY

REBT is a structured approach to emotional problem solving in which the therapist adopts an active-directive approach to helping clients solve their own problems. REBT is multimodal in nature in that therapists use and encourage their clients to use a variety of cognitive, imaginal, behavioral, and emotive-evocative techniques to facilitate therapeutic change. Rational emotive behavior therapists consider that the bulk of therapeutic change is achieved by clients in their daily lives rather than inside therapy sessions. As such, therapists routinely encourage their clients to carry out homework assignments that are individually designed to help them put into practice what they have learned within therapy sessions.

Part II

PRACTICE

The following discussion provides a brief overview of the basic REBT treatment process, as summarized in Table 2. For the purpose of illustration, we assume that you will be dealing with your client's emotional problems one at a time. We thus restrict ourselves to specifying the treatment process as it pertains to a given client problem. Once again, it is important to point out that the actual clinical situation may be far more complex than is indicated in this brief analysis.

Before beginning the treatment process outlined in the following pages, it is important first to greet the client and settle any practical issues that may be of concern (e.g., fees and scheduling of appointments).

TABLE 2 The Rational Emotive Behavioral Treatment Sequence

Step 1: Ask for a Problem

Step 2: Define and Agree upon the Target Problem

Step 3: Agree upon a Goal with Respect to the Problem as Defined

Step 4: Ask for a Specific Example of the Target Problem

Step 5: Assess C

Step 6: Assess A

Step 7: Agree upon a Goal with Respect to the Problem as Assessed

Step 8: Help Your Client to See the Link between the Problem as Defined Goal and the Problem as Assessed Goal

Step 9: Identify and Assess any Meta-emotional Problems If Relevant

Step 10: Teach the B–C connection

Step 11: Assess iB

Step 12: Connect iB and C

Step 13: Question iB and rB

Step 14: Prepare Your Client to Deepen Conviction in Rational Beliefs

Step 15: Check the Validity of A

Step 16: Negotiate a Homework Assignment

Step 17: Check Homework Assignments

Step 18: Facilitate the Working-through Process

Note. A = activating event (and inferences); B = belief; iB = irrational belief; rB = rational belief; C = consequence of irrational belief

Step 1 | Ask for a Problem

After you discuss the necessary practicalities, we suggest that you establish the problem-solving orientation of REBT immediately by asking your client what problem she would like to discuss first. Establishing the *target problem* communicates a number of messages to the client. First, it emphasizes that you are both there to get a job done (i.e., to help the client overcome her emotional problems). Second, it illustrates that REBT is an efficient and focused approach to emotional problem solving. Third, it indicates that, as a therapist, you are going to be active and direct your client immediately to a discussion of her problems.

Client's choice versus client's most serious problem

You can adopt two basic strategies when asking your client to focus on a target problem. In the first case, you ask your client to choose the issue ("What would you like to work on first?"). The client's selection may or may not be her most serious problem. In the second case, you ask your client to start with her most serious problem ("What are you most bothered about in your life right now?").

When your client does not identify a target problem

What can you do if your client does not identify a target problem? (This situation often arises when your "client" is a fellow mental health practitioner with whom you are conducting a peer counseling session during REBT training.) First, let your client know that she does not have to choose a serious problem. Tell her that it is perfectly in order to start the process with an issue that is impeding her in some slight way. Remind her that there is always something

13

to work on because human beings usually operate at a less than optimal level of functioning. Encourage your client to identify *feelings* or *behaviors* she would like to decrease or increase.

Another, more indirect, way of helping your client disclose a target problem is to ask what she would like to achieve from therapy. When your client articulates a goal, you could then ask for ways in which she is currently not achieving this goal. This approach may well lead to a discussion of feelings and/or behaviors that your client identifies as impediments. You could then explore these impediments further without necessarily labeling them problems. The word *problem* serves to discourage some clients from becoming engaged in a problem-focused therapy such as REBT. If this is the case, use a term that is more acceptable (e.g., difficulties, challenges).

| Define and Agree upon
the Target Problem

The nature of your client's problem is often obvious after an initial discussion. If this is the case, you may proceed to assess the problem (Steps 5 through 9). However, when your client's target problem is unclear, or when he has disclosed a number of problems, the two of you should come to an agreement on the nature of the problem and/or which problem to work on first.

Arriving at a common understanding of the problem and agreeing to work on it is an important therapeutic step in REBT in that it strengthens the therapeutic alliance. Doing so enables you and your client to work as a team and helps your client to feel understood and have confidence that you know what you are doing.

Distinguish between an emotional and a practical problem

As Bard (1980) has noted, REBT is a method of psychotherapy that helps clients overcome their *emotional* problems and not their *practical* problems. Of course, clients often have emotional problems about their practical problems, and these may well become the focus of therapeutic exploration. Also, as clients' emotional problems (e.g., anxiety) are addressed, their practical problems (e.g., lack of finances) may also be solved, even though the therapeutic exploration does not expressly deal with such issues (Ellis, 2002). In any case, it is important to help your client to understand this distinction.

Target unhealthy but not healthy negative emotions

In Part I, we distinguished between unhealthy and healthy negative emotions. Do not encourage your client to change healthy negative emotions; these healthy reactions to negative life events will help your client (a) adjust positively to the negative A, (b) cope better with that A, or (c) change the A in more constructive ways. However, do target for change unhealthy negative emotions (i.e., those that stem from irrational beliefs). Help your client to understand the difference between these two types of negative emotions. The question "How is this a problem for you?" will often lead to a useful discussion and help you and your client to identify and define a "real" emotional problem.

Operationalize vague problems

When your client discusses his target problem in vague or confusing terms, it is important that you help him operationalize the problem. For example, if your client says, "My wife is a pain in the ass," help him to specify what this statement means in operational terms (e.g., "What is it your wife does that leads you to conclude that she is a pain in the ass, and how do you feel when she acts this way?").

If you do this, you will find that you are beginning to formulate the problem in ABC terms. The practical problem (or A) is the wife's behavior that makes her "a pain in the ass"; the emotional problem (or C) is the disturbed, unhealthy emotion (e.g., damning anger) your client feels when his wife acts poorly.

Focus on helping your client change C, not A

A common difficulty you may face at this point is that your client may wish to change A rather than his feelings (C) about A. As noted earlier, changing the A is a practical solution; changing the C is the emotional solution. If you encounter this difficulty, you can use a number of strategies to encourage your client to change C before attempting to change A:

1. You can help your client to see that he can change A more effectively if he is not emotionally disturbed about the problems at C.

2. It may be that your client already knows how to change A but cannot do so at this time. If this is the case, it is important to help him understand that the reason he cannot use his productive problem-solving strategies to change A is that he probably is emotionally disturbed about A.

3. If your client does not yet have productive problem-solving strategies in his repertoire to change A, you can often encourage him to focus on his problems at C by showing him that he will learn such strategies if he is not emotionally disturbed about A.

When you still have not identified a problem

If at this stage you still have not reached an agreement with your client concerning the nature of the problem, you can suggest that he keep a *problem diary*. Encourage your client to monitor his disturbed feelings during the following week and suggest that he make written notes of what these feelings are, as well as when and where he experiences them.

Step 3 | Agree upon a Goal with Respect to the Problem as Defined

Once a target problem has been selected and both you and your client broadly agree on the nature of this problem, the next step is to choose a goal in line with the problem as defined. (As we shall see in Step 7, after the problem has been assessed, this goal may change.) Once a goal has been selected, ensure that your client has a realistic chance of achieving it and that it will not reinforce her existing problems.

When discussing goal selection with your client, keep in mind the distinction between *long-term goals* and *short-term goals*. Your client may choose a short-term goal that may in the long term be self-defeating and therefore irrational (e.g., in the case of an anorexic client, the desire to lose more weight). Therefore, encourage your client to take a longer term perspective when choosing goals for change and to make a commitment to carrying out the hard work to achieve them.

Step 4 | Ask for a Specific Example of the Target Problem

In defining and agreeing upon the target problem, it is important that you be as specific as you can. Because your client experiences his emotional problems and holds related irrational beliefs in specific contexts, being specific will help you to obtain reliable and valid data about A, B, and C. Giving your client a plausible rationale for specificity is a good idea, especially if he tends to discuss his target problems in vague terms. Help him to understand that being specific about the problem will help him deal more constructively with it in the situations about which he is disturbed. A good way of modeling specificity for your client is to ask for a recent or typical example of the target problem (e.g., "When is the last time A happened?").

If, after repeated attempts, your client is still unable to provide you with a specific example of the target problem, this may be evidence that he has a meta-emotional problem (e.g., shame) about his original emotional problem (e.g., anxiety). If you suspect this is the case, do not assume that you are correct: Test your hypothesis. (See Step 9 for further discussion of this point.)

Step 5 | Assess C

At this stage, you may assess C or A, depending on which element of the target problem your client raises first. For the purpose of this discussion, we will first consider issues involved in the assessment of C.

Check again for an unhealthy negative emotion

In assessing C, remember that your client's emotional problem will be an unhealthy (disturbed) negative emotion, not a healthy (undisturbed) negative emotion. As noted earlier, an unhealthy negative emotion differs from a healthy negative emotion in that the former usually involves a great deal of emotional pain, motivates one to behave in a self-defeating manner, blocks one from achieving one's goals, and leads to unrealistic thinking.

Table 1 in Part I lists words used in REBT theory to distinguish between these two types of negative emotion. Although these distinctions are important, you should not necessarily expect your client to use this terminology in the same way that you do. For example, she may talk about *anxiety* when she is actually experiencing *concern*, or vice versa (Dryden, 1986). It is important that you identify an unhealthy negative emotion and that you and your client use the same language when referring to it. You may either encourage your client to adopt the REBT terminology of emotion, or you may choose to adopt her use of feeling language. Whatever course you take, be consistent in your vocabulary throughout therapy.

Focus on an emotional C

We recognize that C may be emotional, behavioral, or cognitive. If your client identifies or discusses a behavioral or cognitive C, then look for the emotional C that is associated with the behavioral or cognitive C. For example, dysfunctional behaviors are often defensive in nature and exist to help clients avoid experiencing certain unhealthy negative emotions; therefore, encourage your client to avoid dealing with dysfunctional behaviors and focus instead on unhealthy negative emotions. Thus, if your client wishes to stop smoking, regard smoking as a defensive behavior and encourage her to identify the problematic emotions she might experience were she to refrain from smoking. We suggest that you also adopt this strategy if your client identifies her problem as procrastination or some other kind of avoidance behavior.

Clarify C

If your client identifies a vague C, there are a number of specific techniques you can use to clarify its nature. For example, you can use imagery methods or Gestalt exercises such as the empty chair technique (Passons, 1975) or Gendlin's (1978) focusing technique. When Ellis's clients experience difficulty in identifying a specific emotion, he encourages them to "Take a wild guess," a method that yields surprisingly useful information about C.

Understand that frustration is an A, not a C

Your client may talk about feeling frustrated at C. Some REBT therapists consider frustration to be an activating event (A) rather than a feeling (Trexler, 1976). As a C, frustration in REBT theory is usually regarded as a healthy negative emotion experienced by your client when her goals are blocked. However, when your client says she feels frustrated, it is possible that she is referring to an unhealthy negative emotion. One way of telling whether your client's frustration is a healthy or an unhealthy negative emotion is to ask if the feeling is bearable. If your client says the feeling is unbearable, then it may well be that she is experiencing an unhealthy negative emotion (e.g., rage) that should be targeted for change.

Avoid pitfalls in assessing C

There are a number of pitfalls in assessing your client's problematic emotions at C. The following suggestions will help you avoid them:

1. Do not ask questions that reinforce the assumption that A causes C. Novice REBT therapists frequently ask their clients, "How does the situation make you feel?" An alternative question that does not imply A causes C is "How do you feel about the situation?"

2. Do not accept vague descriptions of feelings such as "bad," "upset," "miserable," and so forth. When your client uses vague terms, help her to clarify exactly what she feels at C. (See Table 1 in Part I for discriminations among negative emotions.) Also, do not accept statements such as "I feel trapped" or "I feel rejected" as descriptions of emotions occurring at C. Recognize that we do not have a feeling called *trapped* or *rejected*. These terms refer to combinations of A, B, and C factors, and it is important to distinguish among these three and ensure that your client's C statements actually do refer to emotions. For example, if your client says, "I feel rejected," help her to recognize that she may have been rejected at point A. Then ask how she felt about the rejection at point C (e.g., "hurt," "ashamed").

Step 6 | Assess A

If you have chosen first to assess C, your next step will be to assess A. As noted earlier, A refers to activating events that may be regarded as confirmable reality (i.e., your client's descriptions of A can be confirmed as accurate by neutral observers). However, in this book, A will also stand for your client's personally significant inferences or interpretations about the activating event.

Be specific in assessing A

As with assessments of C, be as specific as you can when you assess A. For instance, ask for the last time A occurred, a typical example of A, or the most relevant example your client can recall.

Identify the part of A that triggers B

While you are assessing A, help your client to identify the most relevant part of A (i.e., the part that triggers his irrational belief at B, which, in turn, largely determines his unhealthy negative emotion at C). This most relevant part of A is also known as the *critical A*. Sometimes identifying this trigger, or critical A, can be complicated by inferences your client makes about the situation. You can pinpoint the most important of these by using *inference chaining*, a technique that helps you to clarify how your client's inferences are linked.

For example, imagine a client who is anxious at point C. Your first inquiry concerning what he is anxious about reveals that he is due to give a class presentation. Now your task is to find out what it is about giving a class presentation that is anxiety provoking in your client's mind:

Therapist:	What is it about giving the presentation that you are anxious about?
Client:	Well, I may not do a very good job.
Therapist:	Let's assume for the moment that you don't. Now what's anxiety provoking in your mind about that?
Client:	Well, if I don't do a good job in class, then my teacher will give me a poor grade.
Therapist:	Let's assume that as well. What would you be anxious about there?
Client:	That I might flunk the course.
Therapist:	And if you did?
Client:	Oh, my God. I couldn't face my father.
Therapist:	If you told your father that you had failed, what would be anxiety provoking about that in your mind?
Client:	I can just see my father now—he would be devastated.
Therapist:	And how would you feel if that happened?
Client:	Oh, my God, that would be terrible. I really couldn't stand to see my father cry—I'd feel so very sorry for him.

Your client initially identified giving the class presentation as the A. However, inference chaining has uncovered your client's fearful anticipation of his father's devastation upon hearing of the client's presumed failure. To test whether this aspect of A is in fact the most relevant factor in your client's emotional problem, you could write down the inference chain and review it with your client, asking him to identify which aspect of the chain he feels is the most important to him. Another way of finding out whether the new aspect of A is central is to manipulate A and check your client's responses at C. For example, you might say to your client, "Let's suppose you told your father you flunked the course, and he wasn't devastated—in fact, he coped quite well with the news. Would that have any impact on your anxiety about giving the class presentation?" If the client states that it would, you may be more confident that you have assessed the problem correctly. If your client states that he would still be anxious, then it is clear that the prospect of seeing his father's distress (at A) is not the most important factor in the anxiety problem.

Once you have helped your client to identify the critical A, it is important to reassess any changes in his feelings at C since the initial analysis of the problem. For example, assuming that the new A in the case just cited is indeed the central factor, it would be important to encourage your client to see that his anxiety is more closely associated with the overwhelming pity he would feel at C for his father than with any general fears of failure he might have. In terms of treatment, then, two directions would be possible: The first would involve focusing on the client's feelings of anxiety at C about the prospect of his father's emotional devastation. The second would involve asking your client to assume that the new A (the father's devastation) had already taken place, then deal with the feelings of pity that would presumably occur at C. This example demonstrates that your client's feelings, as well as his inferences, can be linked. (For a fuller discussion of inference chaining, see Neenan and Dryden, 1999.)

Remember that A can refer to many things

It is important to keep in mind that, in our view, A might be a thought, an inference, an image, a sensation, or a behavior, as well as an event that can be confirmed by neutral observers. A can refer to past, present, or future events. Your client's feelings at C may also serve as an A. For example, your client may feel guilt at C. This guilt may then serve as a new A, and your client may feel ashamed (a new C) about feeling guilty. Your client may indeed have such a meta-emotional problem about his original emotional problem, although this is not always the case. Determining the existence of meta-emotional problems requires careful and open-minded assessment (see Step 9).

Assume temporarily that A is true

When you assess A, you may discover that your client's critical A is a clear distortion of reality. If this is the case, you may be tempted to question A. Resist this temptation. Rather, at this stage you should encourage your client to assume temporarily that A is correct. For example, in the case previously described, it is not important to determine whether the client's father would truly be devastated by news of the client's failure. What is important is that you encourage your client to assume that A is correct in order to help him identify more accurately the irrational beliefs about the A that have led to his feelings at C. Later in the treatment sequence (at Step 15), you will have an opportunity to check whether A is likely to be true.

Avoid pitfalls in assessing A

There are a number of pitfalls in assessing A. The following suggestions can help you to avoid them:

1. Do not obtain too much detail about A. Allowing your client to talk at length about A can discourage you both from retaining a problem-solving approach to overcoming emotional difficulties. If your client does provide too much detail, try to abstract the salient theme or summarize what you understand to be the major aspect of A. Interrupt your client tactfully and reestablish an REBT-driven assessment focus. For example, you could say, "I think you may be giving me more detail than I require. What was it about the situation that you were most upset about?"

2. Discourage your client from describing A in vague terms. As in the case of assessing C, get as clear and specific an example of A as you can. (An example of a vague A would be the statement "My wife reacted negatively to me." In contrast, a specific A would be "My wife called me a jerk when I told her I cried at the movie last night.")

3. Discourage your client from talking about several A's at one time. In REBT, it is important for you to work on one A at a time; therefore, encourage your client to deal with the A he considers to best illustrate the context in which he makes himself disturbed. Explain that you will deal with the other A's at a later date.

When you still have not identified A

If at this stage your client has still not identified a clear A, encourage him to keep a diary during the time before his next session. In this diary, he can record examples of activating events about which he makes himself disturbed.

Step 7

Agree upon a Goal with Respect to the Problem as Assessed

Once you have assessed the A and C elements of your client's presenting problem, you will often discover that the problem as assessed is different from the one you and your client have defined (Step 3). For example, say your client defines her problem as being overweight and states that her goal is to achieve and maintain a specific target weight. However, when her overeating is assessed, it is discovered that she becomes anxious and overeats when she is bored. At this point, your client's goal with respect to the problem as assessed would involve dealing more constructively with the feeling of boredom so that she does not use the counterproductive strategy of overeating. Thus you may encourage your client to feel concerned (rather than anxious) about being bored and to use that feeling of concern to deal with boredom in more constructive ways. So, at the assessment stage, encourage your client to select as a goal a healthy negative emotion and help her to understand why such an emotion is a realistic and constructive response to a negative activating event at A.

Consider your client's motivation to change C

Sometimes a client will experience unhealthy negative emotions that she is not motivated to change. This lack of motivation can result when your client does not recognize the destructive nature of the emotion she is experiencing. This situation occurs most frequently in the case of anger; it also sometimes happens in the cases of guilt and depression. We therefore recommend that you assess your client's understanding of the dysfunctionality or self-defeating nature of the target emotion (C). This process can begin at Step 5, but it is essential at the problem assessment stage. If your client does not

31

understand why her emotion is unhealthy, spend as much time as necessary helping her to understand this point. Basically, this can be accomplished in three steps:

1. Help your client to assess the consequences of the unhealthy negative emotion. What happens when she feels this way? Does she act constructively? Does she act self-defeatingly? Does she stop herself from acting appropriately?

2. Point out that the goal is to replace the unhealthy negative emotion with the corresponding healthy negative emotion. Getting this point across may be difficult, especially if your client has rigid ideas about the ways she is supposed to feel. However, if provided with appropriate models, your client will usually be able to understand that one can experience the healthy emotion in any given situation.

3. Finally, assess what the consequences would be if your client felt the corresponding healthy emotion in the same situation. Because she has probably not considered such a change, help her to imagine how she would act and how the outcome would be different if she did experience the healthy emotion in the context of the activating event. Compare the outcomes of both healthy and unhealthy negative emotions. Your client will usually understand the advantages of the healthy emotion, and this will increase her motivation to change C.

Avoid pitfalls when agreeing upon goals with respect to the problem as assessed

Several pitfalls need to be avoided when agreeing upon goals after the client's problem has been assessed. The following suggestions will be helpful in doing so:

1. Do not accept your client's goal statements when they express the wish to experience less of an unhealthy negative emotion (e.g., "I want to feel less anxious" or "I want to feel less guilty"). According to rational emotive behavioral theory, the presence of an unhealthy negative emotion (e.g., anxiety or guilt) indicates that your client is holding an irrational belief, albeit in a less intense manner. As such, you are advised to help your client distinguish between the unhealthy negative emotion and its healthy negative counterpart. Encourage your client to set the latter emotion as her goal. She can therefore choose to feel con-

cerned instead of anxious, and remorseful instead of guilty or self-downing.

2. Do not accept goals indicating that your client wishes to feel neutral, indifferent, or calm about adverse events about which it would be rational to feel healthy negative emotions (e.g., disappointment). Emotions indicating indifference (e.g., calmness when an unfortunate event occurs) mean that your client does not have a rational belief about the event in question, whereas, in reality, she probably would prefer that the event had not happened. If you go along with your client's goal to feel calm or indifferent about a negative event, you will encourage her to deny the existence of her desires rather than to think rationally.

3. For similar reasons, do not accept your client's goal to experience positive feelings about a negative A. It is unrealistic for your client to feel happy, for example, when she is faced with a negative life event that she would prefer not to encounter (e.g., a loss or failure). If you accept your client's goal to feel positive about a negative event, you will encourage her to believe that it is good that the negative A occurred. By doing this, you will once again be discouraging your client from thinking rationally. To reiterate an earlier point, when you encourage your client to experience healthy negative emotions in the face of unpleasant life events, you help her to come to terms with or change her situation.

4. Finally, do not accept vague goals (e.g., "I want to be happy"). The more specific you can encourage your client to be in setting goals (e.g., "What specific things would you like to achieve in your life that will help to make you happy?"), the more likely she will be motivated to do the hard work of changing her irrational beliefs in the service of achieving these goals.

Step 8 | Help Your Client to See the Link between the Problem as Defined Goal and the Problem as Assessed Goal

Because there have been two goal-setting stages (Steps 3 and 7), your client may become confused as to how different goals have emerged. (Of course, the goals may be the same if the problems have remained the same at Steps 3 and 7.) If the former is the case, do not assume that your client will automatically see the link between these two goal-setting stages, but help him to understand that the problem as assessed goal is based on a more detailed understanding of his problems (e.g., through inference chaining) than was attempted at Step 3.

Step 9 | Identify and Assess Any Meta-emotional Problems If Relevant

Clients frequently have meta-emotional problems about their original emotional problems (e.g., anger about feeling depressed). Another way of stating this step is as follows: Does the client have secondary emotional problems about her primary emotional problems? If your client's original problem is anxiety, you may ask, "How do you feel about feeling anxious?" to determine whether your client does in fact have a meta-emotional problem about her original problem of anxiety.

Know when to work on the meta-emotional problem first

If any of the following three conditions are met, we suggest that you first focus attention on your client's meta-emotional problem:

1. Your client's meta-emotional problem interferes significantly with the work you are trying to do on her original problem. Such interference might take place either in the session or in the client's outside life.

2. From a clinical perspective, the meta-emotional problem is the more important of the two.

3. Your client can see the sense of working on her meta-emotional problem first.

You may need to present a plausible rationale for starting with the meta-emotional problem first. If, after you have presented your rationale, your client still wishes to work on her original problem first, then do so. To do otherwise may threaten the productive therapeutic alliance you have by now established.

Check for an emotional problem about a healthy negative emotion

When you have assessed your client's *stated* original problem, you may decide that she is in fact experiencing a healthy negative emotion (e.g., sadness in response to an important loss). If so, check to see whether your client has an emotional problem with this healthy emotion. For example, your client may feel ashamed about feeling sad. If this is the case, work to reach an agreement that the meta-emotional problem (shame) will be the client's target problem and then carry out an ABC assessment of this agreed-upon problem.

Assess the presence of shame

As noted earlier, if your client is reluctant to disclose that she has an emotional problem, she may feel ashamed about having the problem or disclosing it to a therapist. When you suspect that this might be the case, ask your client how she would feel if she did have an emotional problem about the activating event you are discussing. If the client says she would feel ashamed, agree with her to work on shame as the target problem before encouraging her to disclose the original problem she had in mind.

Step 10 | Teach the B–C Connection

By now you will have assessed the A and C elements of your client's original problem or meta-problem. The next step is to teach the B–C connection—the notion that your client's emotional problem is determined largely by his beliefs rather than by the activating event (A) you have already assessed. Carrying out this step is critical. Unless your client understands that his emotional problem is determined by his beliefs, he will not understand why you want to assess his beliefs during the next step of the treatment process. Using an example unrelated to your client's problem can often help to explain the concept. Other exercises and metaphors to help teach the idea are detailed in the REBT texts listed in the reference section of this book (e.g., Ellis & Dryden, 1997; Walen et al., 1992).

Step 11 | Assess iB

While assessing B, keep in mind the distinction between your client's rational beliefs (rB) and irrational beliefs (iB), and help her to understand the difference between these two kinds of thinking.

Assess both premise and derivative forms

In Part I, we argued that your client's beliefs can be divided into a premise and certain derivatives from this premise. At this stage of the process, you should carefully assess your client's irrational beliefs. As you do so, assess both the premise form (dogmatic musts, absolute shoulds, have-tos, oughts, etc.) and the three main derivatives from the premise: (a) awfulizing, (b) low frustration tolerance (LFT), and (c) depreciation of self, others, and/or life conditions. As you do this, you can either teach and use the REBT terms for these processes or use your client's own language, ensuring that her terms accurately reflect irrational beliefs. Base your decision on your client's feedback concerning which of these strategies will be the most useful to her.

Remember the three basic musts

While assessing your client's irrational beliefs, keep in mind the three basic musts outlined in Part I: demands about self, demands about others, and demands about world/life conditions.

Distinguish between absolute shoulds and other shoulds

While you are assessing the premise form of your client's irrational beliefs, she may use the word *should*. This word has several different meanings in the English language. Most expressions of the word *should* are unrelated to your client's emotional problems. These include shoulds of preference ("You *should* preferably treat your children with respect"); empirical shoulds ("When two parts of hydrogen and one part of oxygen are mixed, you *should* get water"); and shoulds of recommendation ("You *should* go and see that excellent play at the local theater").

Rational emotive behavioral theory hypothesizes that only *absolute shoulds* are related to emotional disturbance. If your client finds the different meanings confusing, it may be helpful to substitute the word *must* in cases where an irrational belief in its premise form may be operative. (Compare, for instance, "I *should* be admired by my colleagues" with "I *must* be admired by my colleagues.") It is Ellis's and our clinical experience that the word *must* conveys the meaning of absolute demandingness better than the word *should*. In particular, help your client to distinguish between absolute shoulds and shoulds of preference.

Use questions in assessing irrational beliefs

When you assess your client's irrational beliefs, use questions. A standard question that REBT therapists frequently ask is "What were you telling yourself about A to make yourself disturbed at C?" This type of *open-ended question* has both advantages and disadvantages. The main advantage in using this type of inquiry is that you are unlikely to put words in your client's mouth concerning the content of her belief. The main disadvantage is that your client will be unlikely to respond by articulating an irrational belief. Rather, she is most likely to give you further inferences about A—ones that may well be less relevant than the critical A pinpointed at Step 6.

Imagine, for example, that your client is particularly anxious that other people will think her a fool if she stammers in public. Asking her, "What were you telling yourself about other people's criticism to make yourself disturbed at C?" might yield the response "I thought they wouldn't like me." Note that this thought is in fact an inference, and that you still do not know what your client's irrational belief is. In this instance, you want to help the client to understand that her statement does not describe an irrational belief; you also want to educate her to look further for her irrational belief about A. You can do this by judiciously combining the use of open-ended questions with some didactic explanation.

What other kinds of open-ended questions can you use when assessing your client's irrational beliefs? Walen et al. (1992) list a number of possibilities, such as "What was going through your mind?"; "Were you aware of any thoughts in your head?"; "What was on your mind then?"; and "Are you aware of what you were thinking at that moment?" Again, note that your client may not spontaneously disclose irrational beliefs in response to these questions; she may well need further help of a didactic nature.

An alternative to asking open-ended questions at A is to ask *theory-driven questions* (i.e., questions that are directly derived from rational emotive behavioral theory). For example, to elicit an answer specifying a must (i.e., a premise), you might ask, "What demand were you making about other people's criticism to make yourself disturbed at point C?" To assess the presence of a derivative of a must, you might ask, "What kind of person did you think you were for stammering and incurring other people's criticism?"

The advantage of theory-driven questions is that they orient your client to look for her irrational beliefs. The danger is that you may be putting words in your client's mouth and encouraging her to look for irrational beliefs that she may not have. However, you will minimize this danger if you have already established that your client has an unhealthy negative emotion at point C.

Step 12 | Connect iB and C

After you have accurately assessed your client's irrational beliefs in the form of both premise and derivatives, ensure that your client understands the connection between his irrational beliefs (iB) and his disturbed emotions at point C before proceeding to question these beliefs. Thus you might ask, "Can you understand that, as long as you demand that other people must not criticize you, you are bound to make yourself anxious about this happening?" or "Can you see that, as long as you believe that you are no good for being regarded by others as a fool, you will be anxious about being criticized?" If your client says yes, you can then attempt to elicit the B–C connection (e.g., "So, in order to change your feeling of anxiety to one of concern, what do you need to change first?").

Eliciting this connection is likely to be more productive than telling your client that such a connection exists. If your client says he understands that he needs to change his belief in order to change his feeling, this will indicate that he has grasped the concept. If he does not see the connection, spend time helping him to understand it before beginning to dispute his irrational beliefs.

Step 13 | Question iB and rB

After conducting a thorough assessment of the target problem, identifying and assessing any meta-emotional problems, and teaching the iB–C connection, your next step is to begin to question your client's beliefs, both irrational and rational.

Work to achieve the goals of questioning

The major goal of questioning at this stage of the REBT treatment process is to encourage your client to understand that her irrational belief is unproductive (i.e., it leads to self-defeating emotions), illogical (i.e., it does not make sense), and unrealistic (i.e., it is inconsistent with reality) and that the alternative to this belief (i.e., a rational belief) is productive, logical, and realistic.

If you succeed in helping your client to achieve such an understanding at this stage, do not assume that her conviction in the rational belief will be strong. Help your client to distinguish between *light conviction* and *deep conviction* in a rational belief. Also encourage her to see that, at this stage, even a light conviction in an alternative rational belief (i.e., intellectual understanding) is a sign of progress, albeit insufficient in itself to promote emotional and behavioral change.

With specific regard to the target problem, the goals of questioning are to help your client understand the following:

1. Musts: Help your client to understand that there is no evidence in support of her absolute demand, whereas evidence does exist for her preferences. (As Ellis often says: "There are most likely no absolute musts in the universe.") Help your client to see that if her musts were true, then what she was demanding would have to happen—an idea that is patently ridiculous.

47

2. Awfulizing: Help your client to understand that what she has defined as awful (i.e., 100 percent bad) is magical nonsense, and, in reality, all experience lies within a 0–99.99 percent range of badness. Another way of addressing this issue is to show the client that "awful" means her personal world has been shattered beyond repair (which is untrue) and that no good can possibly ever come from the "awful" event (which is also untrue).

3. Low frustration tolerance (LFT): Help your client to understand that when she holds an LFT belief and thinks she cannot stand something, she believes that she will die, disintegrate, or forfeit her capacity for future happiness. All three possibilities are remote, even when she keeps telling herself, "I can't stand it."

4. Depreciation: Help your client to understand that when she depreciates herself, others, or life conditions, she is giving herself, others, and life conditions a negative global rating. Not only is such a rating untrue (e.g., "If it were true that I *am* bad, then this would be my essence, and I could not possibly do good things"), but it is also illogical. In other words, it rates the whole of something on the basis of a part (e.g., "You are bad because you acted badly") and yields poor emotional, behavioral, and cognitive consequences.

Once the irrational belief has been questioned, your client needs to learn to replace it with a new, rational belief (like the self-acceptance belief just mentioned). Work together to construct a rational belief that is most adaptive with respect to the A. After you have helped your client construct an alternative rational belief, question it logically, empirically, and pragmatically to confirm its rational status. It is much better for your client to see for herself the evidence that rational beliefs are more likely to help her goal-directed behavior than for you to tell her so. Irrational and rational beliefs can also be questioned concurrently instead of consecutively. When you choose the concurrent method, you can ask your client which belief is true and which is false, which is logical and which is illogical, and which is helpful and which is unhelpful. Ensure that you elicit from your client the reasons for each answer.

Rational beliefs in REBT consist of preferences and their derivatives and act as flexible alternatives to rigid musts and their derivatives:

1. Preferences: Help your client to understand that preferences are flexible and nondogmatic in nature and suggest what we want

to happen (e.g., "I want a new car") and what we do not want to happen (e.g., "I don't want my partner to leave me"). In order for your client to grasp the rationality of a preferential statement, it is important for her to state it in its complete form: "I want a new car, *but* there's no reason why I must have one" and "I don't want my partner to leave me, *but* there's no reason why he must not leave me." The danger in expressing a preferential statement only in its partial form is that it can easily be converted to a dogmatic demand (e.g., "I want a new car [and therefore I must have one]"). The stronger the preference, the more tempting it can become for us to change it into a demand.

2. Anti-awfulizing: Help your client to understand that anti-awfulizing refers to accepting negative life conditions as bad or tragic but not the end of the world (e.g., "Things are pretty bleak in my life at the moment, but not awful"). Acceptance does not mean liking negative events or showing passivity in the face of them; individuals attempt to alter those aspects of reality that they discern can be changed or modified. Anti-awfulizing also implies that some good can sometimes come from the bad things that happen to us and that, although our lives may have been battered by these bad things, they have not been shattered beyond repair by them.

3. Higher frustration tolerance (HFT): Help your client to understand that HFT means learning to increase her ability to withstand discomfort and hardship in life and realizing that she can still enjoy some measure of happiness and stability (e.g., "I certainly don't like the pressure I'm under at the moment, but I can learn to deal with it constructively instead of blowing my top"). Acquiring HFT helps your client to endure the effort involved in reaching her goals.

4. Acceptance of self, others, and life conditions: Help your client to understand that acceptance refers to seeing herself and others as fallible and in a state of flux. Therefore, it is futile to give herself or others a single global rating, as this rating can never fully describe or encompass the totality of what it means to be human (e.g., "Even though my partner left me, I refuse to condemn myself as worthless because of it. I am too complex to be rated in any way"). She can choose to rate her and others' traits or actions, if this is deemed to be helpful in some way (e.g., "Being impulsive can be very counterproductive at times, so I will learn to take things slower before making a decision"), but it is not

realistic, logical, or helpful to rate the whole of a person on the basis of a part of him or her. Also, help your client to see that acceptance of life conditions involves viewing those conditions as being composed of a complex mixture of negative, positive, and neutral events.

Much later in the treatment process (at a point beyond the scope of this primer), your goal will be to help your client internalize a broad range of rational beliefs so that those beliefs become part of a general philosophy of rational living.

Make good use of questions

Let us assume that you are going to question your client's irrational belief in the form of a must. The first stage in the questioning sequence is to ask for evidence in support of the must. Standard questions designed to accomplish this include the following: "Where is the evidence that you must, under all conditions, be loved?"; "Where is the proof?"; "Is it true that you must?"; and "Where is it written that you must?"

Ensure that your client answers the question you have asked. For example, in response to the question "Why must you succeed?" she might reply, "Because it would bring me advantages if I succeed." Note that your client has not answered the question you actually asked, but has answered a different question, namely, "Why is it *preferable* for you to succeed?" In fact, it is a good idea to anticipate that your client will not immediately provide a correct answer to your question—a fact borne out by our clinical experience.

According to REBT theory, the only correct answer to the question "Why must you succeed?" is "There is no reason why I must succeed, although I very much want to." If your client gives any other answer, you may need to educate her concerning why her answer is either (a) incorrect with respect to the question you have asked or (b) a correct response to a different question. During this process, use a combination of questions and short didactic explanations until your client gives the correct answer and understands and agrees with this answer. (Understanding why the answer is correct is not the same as agreeing with it.)

As part of this process, again help your client to distinguish between her rational and irrational beliefs. One way of doing this would be to write down (on an easel or chalkboard, for example) the following two questions:

1. Why must you succeed?
2. Why is it preferable but not essential for you to succeed?

Ask your client to answer these questions. It is likely that she will give you the same answer to both. If so, help her to see that the reasons she has given constitute evidence for her rational belief but not for her irrational belief. As we have already stressed, help her to understand that the only answer to a question about the existence of musts is, to quote Ellis, "There are most likely no absolute musts in the universe (one's own or the cosmos) . . ." Once this understanding has been achieved, help your client to answer questions regarding the rational nature of her preferences. To finish the quote from Ellis: ". . . only desiderata—things I desire."

Be persistent in questioning premise or derivatives

We noted earlier that it is important to question your client's irrational beliefs in the form of both her premise (must) and at least one of her three derivatives from that premise (awfulizing, low frustration tolerance, or depreciation). However, if you have decided to question the irrational premise before beginning to question a derivative from the premise, persist nondogmatically until you have shown your client that there is no evidence in support of her premise. Similarly, if you have chosen to question your client's rational premise first, show her the evidence in support of her premise before moving on to question a rational derivative from the premise.

Switching from premise to derivative (and from derivative to premise) can be confusing for the client. However, if you have persisted in questioning an irrational premise and it becomes clear that your client is not finding this helpful, you may wish to redirect your focus toward a derivative and then monitor your client's reactions. Some clients find it easier to understand why these derivatives are irrational than why their musts are irrational. In the same way, if your client finds it hard to understand why her preference (premise) is rational, then it may be more enlightening for her to concentrate on discussing a derivative (e.g., self-acceptance) from the premise.

Use a variety of questioning strategies

There are three basic questioning strategies. It is best to use all three if you can.

1. Focus on logic: Your purpose here is to help your client to under-stand why her irrational belief is illogical and her rational belief is logical. Help your client to see that just because she wants some-thing to happen, it does not logically follow that it absolutely must happen. Ask the question "Where is the logic?" rather than "Where is the evidence?" and stress that your client's must about her preference is magical in nature, whereas her preference is based on sound reasoning (i.e., the avoidance of non sequiturs).

2. Focus on empiricism: Your goal here is to show your client that her musts and associated derivatives from these musts are almost always empirically inconsistent with reality. As such, use questions that ask your client to provide evidence in support of her irrational beliefs (e.g., "Where is the evidence?"). For instance, to help your client understand that if there were evi-dence to support her belief that she must succeed, then she would have to succeed no matter what she believed. If she is not succeeding at present, that fact constitutes evidence that her irra-tional belief is empirically inconsistent with reality. With regard to your client's preferences and associated derivatives, show her that these are empirically consistent with reality because, with regard to the example discussed here, she can prove (a) that it is preferable for her to succeed and (b) that she does not have to succeed.

3. Focus on pragmatism: The purpose of focusing on the prag-matic consequences of your client's holding irrational beliefs is to show her that, as long as she believes in her irrational musts and their derivatives, she is going to remain disturbed. Ask questions such as "Where is believing that you must succeed going to get you, other than anxious and depressed?" Help your client to see that by endorsing rational beliefs, the probable con-sequences for her will be reductions in the frequency, intensity, and duration of her emotional upsets.

Use a variety of questioning styles

Although many individual variations are possible, four basic styles of questioning are used to question your client's irrational and rational beliefs.

Socratic style

When you use the Socratic style of questioning, your main task is to ask questions concerning the illogical, empirically inconsistent, and dysfunctional aspects of your client's irrational beliefs and the logical, empirically consistent, and functional aspects of her rational beliefs. The purpose of this style is to encourage your client to think for herself rather than to accept your viewpoint just because you have some authority as a therapist. Although this approach depends mainly on questions, brief explanations designed to correct your client's misconceptions may also be included.

Didactic style

Although REBT therapists prefer the Socratic style, asking questions does not always prove productive. If not, you may have to shift to giving more lengthy didactic explanations concerning why an irrational belief is self-defeating and why a rational belief is more productive. Indeed, you will probably have to use didactic explanations to varying degrees with all of your clients at some point in the treatment process.

When you use didactic explanations, be sure that your client understands what you have been saying by asking her to paraphrase your points. You might say, for example, "I'm not sure whether I'm making myself clear here—perhaps you could put into your own words what you think I've been saying to you." Do not accept without question your client's nonverbal and paraverbal signs of understanding (e.g., head nods, hmm-hmms) as evidence that she has in fact understood you. As one of us (R. D.) often says, "There is no good course without a test!" Such "tests" help your client to become an active participant in, rather than a passive recipient of, didactic explanations of aspects of REBT.

Humorous style

With some clients, a productive way of making the point that there is no evidence for irrational beliefs is to use humor or humorous exaggeration. As Walen et al. (1992) note:

> If the client says, "It's really awful that I failed the test!" the therapist might respond, "You're right! It's not only awful, but I don't see how you're going to survive. That's the worst news I've ever heard! This is so horrendous that I can't bear to talk about it. Let's talk about something else, quick!" Such paradoxical statements frequently point out the senselessness of the irrational belief to the client, and very little further debate may be necessary to make the point. (p. 164)

Use humorous exaggeration as a questioning strategy only if (a) you have established a good relationship with your client, (b) your client has already shown some evidence that she has a sense of humor, and (c) your humorous intervention is directed at the irrationality of the client's belief and *not* at the client as a person.

Self-disclosing style

Another constructive way of questioning your client's irrational beliefs involves therapist self-disclosure. In the *coping model* of self-disclosure, you reveal that (a) you have experienced a problem similar to your client's, (b) you once held an irrational belief similar to your client's, and (c) you changed your belief and no longer have the problem. For example, one of us (W. D.) has used the personal example of overcoming anxiety about stammering in public:

> I disclose that I used to believe "I must not stammer." I stress that this belief increased rather than diminished my anxiety. I then show how I questioned this irrational belief by proving to myself that there was no evidence to support it, then changed it to the following rational belief: "There is no reason why I must not stammer. If I stammer, I stammer. That's unfortunate, but hardly awful." I then describe how I pushed myself to put this rational belief into practice while speaking in public and finally outline the productive effects that I experienced by doing so.

The coping model of self-disclosure contrasts with a *mastery model*. In the latter model, you disclose that you have never experienced a problem similar to your client's because you have always thought rationally about the problem at hand. The mastery model tends to accentuate the differences between you and your client and, in our experience, is less productive than the coping model in encouraging your client to challenge her own irrationality. However, some of your clients will not find even the coping model useful. If this is the case, avoid self-disclosure as a questioning strategy and use other strategies instead.

Be creative

The more experience you gain in questioning irrational and rational beliefs, the more you will develop your own individual style of questioning. Thus you will build up a repertoire of stories, aphorisms, metaphors, and other examples to show your clients why their irrational beliefs are self-defeating and why rational alternatives will promote psychological health.

For example, in working with clients who believe they must not experience panic and could not stand it if they did, one of us (W. D.) uses a technique called the *Terrorist Dispute:*

> I say, "Let's suppose that your parents have been
> captured by radical terrorists, and these radicals
> will release your parents only if you agree to put up
> with 10 panic attacks. Will you agree to these
> terms?" The client almost always says yes. If so, I
> will then say, "But I thought you couldn't stand the
> experience of panic." The client usually replies:
> "Well, but I would do it in order to save my par-
> ents." To which I respond, "Yes, but will you do it
> for your own mental health?"

Another creative questioning strategy is what we call the *Friend Dispute,* an approach that is useful for pointing out to clients the existence of unreasonable self-standards:

> Imagine that your client has failed an important
> test and believes, "I must do well, and I am no
> good if I don't." Ask her whether she would con-
> demn her best friend for a similar failure in the
> same way she condemns herself. Normally, your
> client will say no. If so, point out that she has a dif-
> ferent attitude towards her friend than she has
> towards herself. Suggest that if she chose to be as
> compassionate towards herself as she is towards
> her friend, she would be better able to help herself
> solve her own emotional problems.

We end this section on questioning irrational and rational beliefs with one piece of advice: Before trying to be too creative, master the basics.

Step 14 | Prepare Your Client to Deepen Conviction in Rational Beliefs

Once your client has acknowledged that (a) there is no evidence in support of his irrational beliefs, but there is evidence to support his rational beliefs, (b) it would be more logical for him to think rationally, and (c) his rational beliefs will lead him to more productive emotional results than will his irrational beliefs, then you are in a position to help him deepen his conviction in his rational beliefs.

Point out why weak conviction will not promote change

Start by helping your client to understand why a weak conviction in rational beliefs, although important, is insufficient to promote change. Do this by discussing briefly the REBT view of therapeutic change. Using Socratic questioning and brief didactic explanations (see Step 13), help your client to see that he will strengthen his conviction in his rational beliefs by questioning his irrational beliefs and replacing them with their rational alternatives within and between therapy sessions. Also help your client to understand that this process will require him to *act* against his irrational beliefs as well as to question them cognitively. Establishing this point now will help you later, when you encourage your client to put his new learning into practice through homework assignments (Step 16) and as you facilitate the working-through process (Step 18).

Deal with the "head-gut" issue

As you help your client to think more rationally, he may say something like "I understand my rational belief will help me to achieve my goals, but I don't really believe in it yet" or "I believe it intellectually but not emotionally" or "I believe it in my head but don't feel it in my gut." Indeed, you may wish to bring up this point yourself as a prelude to discussing with your client how he is going to deepen his conviction in his rational belief and weaken his conviction in his irrational one. You might ask, for example, "What do you think you will have to do in order to get your new rational belief into your gut?"

Encourage your client to commit himself to a process of therapeutic change that requires him to question his irrational beliefs repeatedly and forcefully and to practice thinking rationally in relevant life contexts. As described in Step 16, this process will involve undertaking a variety of homework assignments.

Step 15 | Check the Validity of A

In Step 6, we emphasized the importance of encouraging your client to assume temporarily that her A (particularly her critical A) is true, even if it is a clear distortion of reality. This is done to identify the irrational belief (B), which largely determines her unhealthy negative emotion at C. However, once you have helped your client to question her irrational belief and what she needs to do in order to internalize her new rational belief, you can revisit the critical A (located in Step 6) and help your client to check its validity by asking some of the following questions:

- How realistic was your A?
- How else could you have viewed this situation?
- How likely is it that your inference is true?

  Would 12 objective observers conclude that your inference was true?

  If not, what would they have said was a more accurate inference, given all the evidence at hand?

  If you told someone whom you could trust to give an independent opinion of the truth or falsity of your inference, what might this person say to you?

  If someone told you that she had made the same inference about the same situation that you faced, what would you say to this person about the validity of her inference?

  What information do you need to collect in order to check the validity of your inference, and how reliable will such information be?

If your client still adheres to her inferential distortions about A, which, in REBT terms, stem from her irrational belief, return to examining this belief, because it represents the main target of therapeutic questioning. Once this belief has been attenuated or removed, any lingering inferential distortions can be dealt with.

Step 16 | Negotiate a Homework Assignment

Your client is now ready to put his rational belief into practice. Remind him again that the rational emotive behavioral theory of change holds that, in order to deepen his convictions in his rational belief, he needs to practice questioning his irrational belief and strengthen his rational belief in situations that are the same or similar to the activating event already assessed. Help your client to choose from among a wide variety of homework assignments advocated in REBT:

1. Cognitive assignments: These vary in complexity and structure. One typical cognitive assignment would involve having the client practice his newly learned questioning techniques by attempting to convince someone else of their rationality. Another might involve having the client rehearse rational self-statements before confronting a problematic activating event. (See Ellis, 1988, and Ellis & Dryden, 1997, for additional examples.)

2. Imagery assignments: These involve your client's deliberate attempts to change an unhealthy negative emotion to a healthy negative emotion, all the while vividly imagining the troublesome activating event. These assignments are particularly helpful when you wish to encourage your client to become confident enough so that he can carry out an in vivo assignment. (See Maultsby & Ellis, 1974, and Walen et al., 1992, for further discussion.)

3. Emotive-evocative assignments: These involve the client's forcefully and vigorously questioning his irrational beliefs in situations that evoke strong feelings. (See Ellis & Dryden, 1997.)

4. Behavioral assignments: Sometimes known as *in vivo flooding*, these assignments involve having the client confront fully and immediately the troublesome situations about which he makes himself disturbed, while simultaneously questioning forcefully any irrational beliefs in these contexts. If your client is reluctant or refuses to undertake this type of assignment, you can encourage him to choose an alternate task that he feels is challenging, but not overwhelming. However, try to persuade your client to carry out an assignment that involves at least some discomfort. Whatever behavioral assignment you negotiate with your client, ensure that it is both legal and ethical.

Ensure that homework assignments are relevant

Make sure that homework assignments are relevant to the irrational belief targeted for change and that, if the client carries out these assignments, doing so will help him deepen his conviction in the rational alternative (i.e., his rational belief).

Collaborate with your client

While you are discussing appropriate homework assignments, enlist your client's active collaboration in the process. Ensure that he can see the sense of carrying out the homework assignment; that if he does so, the experience will help him to achieve his goals; and that he has some degree of confidence that he will be able to execute the agreed-upon assignment. Maximize the chances that your client will complete the assignment by helping him to specify *when* he will do it, in *which* context, and *how* frequently.

Be prepared to compromise

An ideal homework assignment will involve the client's actively and forcefully questioning his irrational beliefs in the most relevant contexts possible. Try to encourage your client to carry out an ideal assignment. If this is not possible, urge him to (a) question his irrational beliefs in situations that approximate the most relevant A or (b) use imagery and question his irrational beliefs while vividly imagining A. You may find that if your client does these less-than-ideal assignments, he will be more likely later on to a carry out a more challenging or even ideal assignment.

Assess and troubleshoot obstacles

While you are negotiating appropriate homework assignments with your client, help him to specify any obstacles that might serve as impediments to homework completion. Encourage your client to find possible ways of overcoming these obstacles in advance of carrying out each assignment.

Use homework at different times during therapy

For the purpose of discussion, we have focused on homework assignments that involve your client's strengthening his conviction in his rational beliefs. However, you can employ such assignments at any point during the treatment sequence. Specifically, you might encourage your client to execute homework assignments to help him (a) pinpoint his troublesome emotions at C, (b) detect his irrational beliefs at B, and (c) identify the most relevant aspect of A (critical A) about which he has made himself disturbed.

You may also employ homework assignments as part of a process in which you educate your client about the ABC's of REBT. In this case, you could ask your client to read various books (bibliotherapy) or listen to REBT lectures on audiotape. When doing so, choose material that is relevant to your client's problem and that he can readily understand. If no appropriate material is available, you might even create written materials or audiotapes to address your client's particular problem.

Step 17

Check Homework Assignments

Once you have negotiated a particular homework assignment with your client and she has undertaken it, use the beginning of the next session to check what she has learned from the experience. If you fail to do this, you show your client that you do not consider homework assignments to be an important ingredient in the process of change, when, in fact, they are central to it.

Verify that your client faced A

As noted earlier, clients are prone to develop strategies to avoid A's rather than strategies to confront A's and change C's. Homework assignments, at this stage, are primarily designed to solve emotional problems, not practical problems. Therefore, when you check on your client's experience in carrying out an assignment, make sure she actually faced the A she committed herself to confront. If your client has done this, she will usually report that she first made herself disturbed and then made herself undisturbed in the same situation by using the questioning techniques discussed in therapy. If your client has not done so, point this out to her, deal with any obstacles involved, and encourage her to confront the situation once more and use vigorous questioning to make herself undisturbed in that context. If necessary, model appropriate questions and encourage your client to rehearse these in the session and before facing the situation in question.

Verify that your client changed B

If your client reports a successful experience in carrying out the homework assignment, assess whether her success can be attributed to her (a) changing her irrational belief to its rational alternative, (b) changing either A itself or her inferences about A, or (c) using distraction techniques. If your client used the latter two methods, acknowledge her efforts but point out that these methods may not be helpful in the long term. Stress that practical solutions or distractions are only palliative, because if an individual has not learned to change the unhealthy negative emotion associated with the situation, the solution is not a permanent one. If unpleasant or adverse A's are unavoidable, the emotional problem will only reassert itself. Once again, encourage the client to face the situation at A, but this time elicit her commitment that she will question her irrational belief and practice acting on the basis of the new rational belief.

Deal with failure to complete homework assignments

If your client has failed to execute the agreed-upon homework assignment, accept her as a fallible human being and help her to identify the reasons she did not carry out the assignment. Use the ABC framework to encourage your client to focus on possible irrational beliefs that served to prevent her from carrying out the assignment. Assess in particular whether your client held irrational beliefs indicating a philosophy of low frustration tolerance (e.g., "It was too hard"; "I couldn't be bothered"; "I shouldn't have to put this much energy into therapy"). If your client holds such beliefs, encourage her to challenge and change them, then reassign the homework.

Step 18 | Facilitate the Working-through Process

For your client to achieve enduring therapeutic change, he needs to challenge and change his irrational beliefs repeatedly and forcefully in relevant contexts at A. In doing so, he will further strengthen his conviction in rational beliefs and continue to weaken his conviction in irrational ones. The purpose of this working-through process is for your client to integrate rational beliefs into his emotional and behavioral repertoire.

Suggest different homework assignments for the same irrational belief

When your client has achieved some success at questioning his irrational belief in relevant situations at A, suggest that he use different homework assignments to encourage change in the same belief. Doing so serves to teach your client that he can use a variety of methods to question the target irrational belief, as well as other irrational beliefs that may emerge during the course of therapy. In addition, such variety may help to sustain his interest in the change process.

Discuss the nonlinear model of change

Explain that change is nonlinear and that your client will probably experience some difficulties in sustaining his success at questioning his irrational beliefs in a wide range of contexts. Identify possible setbacks and help your client develop ways of handling these setbacks. In particular, help your client to pinpoint and challenge the irrational beliefs that might underpin these relapses (e.g., "I shouldn't have to keep working this hard to change!").

In addition, explain that change can be evaluated on three major dimensions:

1. Frequency: Does your client make himself disturbed less frequently than he did before?
2. Intensity: When your client makes himself disturbed, does he do so with less intensity than before?
3. Duration: When your client makes himself disturbed, does he do so for shorter periods of time than before?

Using these three criteria of change, encourage your client to keep records of his disturbed emotions at point C. At this point, it is also helpful to have your client read *How to Enhance and Maintain Your Rational Emotive Behavior Therapy Gains* (Ellis, 1984b). This booklet includes many useful suggestions to help your client facilitate his own working-through process.

Encourage your client to take responsibility for continued progress

At this stage, you can help your client to develop his own homework assignments to change his target belief and to change other irrational beliefs in different situations. Thus, if your client has been successful at questioning an irrational belief about approval in a work-related situation in which he faces criticism, you could encourage him to question this belief in other situations in which he may encounter criticism (e.g., with strangers or friends). The more your client develops and executes his own homework assignments, the more he will begin to serve as his own therapist. This accomplishment is important because, as an REBT therapist, your long-term goal is to encourage your client to internalize the REBT model of change and to take responsibility for further progress after therapy has ended.

Part III

CASE EXAMPLE

In the final part of this primer, we present actual case material to illustrate the rational emotive behavioral treatment sequence described in Part II. Although a single case cannot illustrate all the points discussed, we believe that the case chosen does cover the most salient issues. In order to demonstrate clearly the steps in the REBT treatment sequence, we deliberately selected a case in which the client responded well to REBT.

The client, Karen, was referred to me (W. D.) by her general practitioner, whom she had consulted for problems of sleeplessness and general tension. At the time of the referral, Karen was 26 years old and worked as a laboratory technician at a local college. She lived at home with her parents, did not have a partner, but did have several close friends of the same sex whom she had recently been avoiding. Karen had never sought therapy before.

Before beginning the treatment process, I greeted Karen and discovered how she came to be referred to me. Then we discussed her expectations for therapy and agreed on a fee appropriate to her situation.

STEP 1   ASK FOR A PROBLEM

After dealing with these initial practicalities, I then asked Karen what problem she would like to start with. She said that she had been having trouble sleeping during the past few months and had been avoiding social contact with other people, including her close friends. She traced the development of these problems back to the end of her relationship with Pete, her fiancé, who had left her for another woman three months earlier.

I commented that Karen had several problems and suggested that we list them so that we could deal with them one by one. Karen thought this was a good idea, and we developed the following problem list:

1. Feelings of hurt about the breakup of my relationship with Pete

2. Avoiding contact with my friends

3. Sleeplessness

4. General tension

I again asked Karen which problem she would like to start with, and she chose the problem of avoiding contact with her friends. This issue thus became the target problem of therapy.

STEP 2   DEFINE AND AGREE UPON THE TARGET PROBLEM

I asked Karen to tell me a little more about the problem, and the following dialogue ensued:

Karen: Well, ever since Pete dumped me, I've just not felt like seeing anyone, least of all my friends. Part of me wants to see them because I miss them very much, but another part of me just wants to hibernate.

W. D.: But let's suppose that you did go to see your friends. What feelings do you think you might experience?

Karen: I'm not sure. I think I would be very uncomfortable.

W. D.: And then what would happen?

Karen: I'd just make some excuse to go home again.

W. D.: So it may be that what you call avoidance of social contact with your friends really has to do with your avoiding uncomfortable feelings that you think you would experience.

Karen: That seems right.

STEP 3   AGREE UPON A GOAL WITH RESPECT TO THE PROBLEM AS DEFINED

Client goal selection at this stage is usually provisional, because information related to the target problem is often insufficient to gain a clear picture of the determinants of the problem.

W. D.:   So what would you like to do about these uncomfortable feelings that you experience?

Karen: Well, it would be helpful to take a closer look at these feelings and see what's going on. I want to choose whether or not to see my friends from a healthier outlook.

W. D.:   That seems like a good idea.

STEP 4   ASK FOR A SPECIFIC EXAMPLE OF THE TARGET PROBLEM

Up to this point, Karen had spoken about the uncomfortable feelings she would experience if she visited her friends. The next step was to anchor the target problem in a specific example in order to move counseling from the general to the concrete.

W. D.:   Can you think of a specific occasion when you experienced these uncomfortable feelings?

Karen: About a week ago I was invited by some friends to go to a party.

W. D.:   Did you accept?

Karen: No. I felt safer at home, hibernating.

W. D.:   That seems a good example to focus upon.

STEP 5   ASSESS C

My hypothesis at this point was that Karen's social avoidance served to help her to avoid negative feelings. I next moved on to obtain a more precise assessment of these feelings.

W. D.:   Now, if you were to go to the party and meet with your close friends and remain with them, and you really let yourself experience those uncomfortable feelings that you mentioned, what kind of feelings would they be?

Karen: I'm not sure.

W. D.:   Well, close your eyes and see yourself with your friends; really try to picture yourself and picture them. Try to imagine that you are with them right now. What are you experiencing?

Karen: *(Pauses.)* It's funny—I feel anxious.

STEP 6   ASSESS A

As shown in the previous step, Karen had been able to identify the feeling of anxiety as the C in the situation. My next step was to use inference chaining to help her define the part of A (critical A) that triggered her anxiety.

W. D.:   Now open your eyes. You seem surprised to learn that you would feel anxious. What do you think you would be anxious about?

Karen: Well, when you asked me to picture my friends, I had an image of them disapproving of me.

W. D.:   For what reason?

Karen: Well, it was as if they were thinking, "She can't be up to much if her fiancé goes off with another woman."

W. D.:   Well, we don't know whether or not they would be thinking that, but let's assume for a moment that you were right. What would be anxiety provoking in your mind if they did think you weren't up to much?

Karen: Well, it would mean they would look down on me.

W. D.:   And what would be anxiety provoking in your mind about that?

Karen: *(Pauses.)* Just that—that they would look down on me.

   [The client's critical A has been located.]

W. D.:   Now, does that seem to explain what those uncomfortable feelings that you mentioned earlier are about?

Karen: Yes, it does.

W. D.:   Right, and as we look at it now with them looking down at you, what feelings go along with that?

Karen: *(Pauses.)* Shame. Yes, I'd feel very ashamed.

Note that Karen's C has changed from anxiety to shame. This frequently happens when the client's disturbed feeling involves anxiety. As shown in Table 1 in Part I, anxiety occurs when the person has an irrational belief about some future threat. When, in the context of exploring the client's A, the therapist asks the client to assume that the threat has occurred, the client's feeling changes to reflect this assumption. For example, Karen would be *anxious* about the prospect that her friends would look down on her, but would feel *ashamed* if that event had actually taken place.

STEP 7   AGREE UPON A GOAL WITH RESPECT TO THE PROBLEM AS ASSESSED

In Step 3, it was agreed that the goal ("I want to choose whether or not to see my friends from a healthier outlook") was based upon the problem as defined. In this step, goal selection was based upon the information revealed about the nature of Karen's anxiety (C) during the assessment of A. I decided to treat Karen's C as shame and thus encouraged her to assume that A (her friends' looking down on her) had actually occurred. My next task was to encourage her to feel disappointed, rather than ashamed, about this situation should it occur (new goal).

W. D.:   Now, as long as you feel ashamed in the face of your friends looking down on you, it makes sense for you to avoid them. Can you see that?

Karen: Yes.

W. D.:   But let's see what alternatives you have about handling the situation where they look down on you. I want to stress, however, that we're assuming for the moment that they *would* look down on you. Realistically, they may very well not, but let's assume that they would. What productive feelings could you strive to experience instead of shame?

Karen: To be indifferent towards them?

W. D.:   But is that realistic? Do you think you could ever be indifferent about what your close friends think of you?

Karen: No, I guess not.

W. D.:   What else could you feel instead of shame?

Karen: I'm not sure.

W. D.:   How about feeling disappointed? My guess is that, if you felt disappointed but not ashamed in the face of them looking down on you, you wouldn't run away, and you would be in a position to try to persuade them that they were wrong to disapprove of you, something you couldn't do if you were ashamed.

Karen: Yes, that makes sense, but how do I get myself to feel disappointed rather than ashamed?

STEP 8   HELP YOUR CLIENT TO SEE THE LINK BETWEEN THE PROBLEM AS DEFINED GOAL AND THE PROBLEM AS ASSESSED GOAL

Because there had been two goal-setting stages (Steps 3 and 7), Karen seemed confused about how two different goals for change had emerged. I attempted to show Karen how they were linked.

W. D.:   The first goal of deciding whether or not to see your friends from an undisturbed viewpoint was agreed upon after just skimming the surface of your problem. When the problem was explored in depth through the use of a specific example, we discovered that you felt ashamed if your friends looked down on you.

Karen: OK, so far so good.

W. D.:   So if you feel disappointed instead of ashamed about your friends looking down on you, you will not be emotionally disturbed about the situation and therefore better able to decide if you want to see your friends or not. That's how the two goals are linked.

Karen: So if I try to feel disappointed about the situation instead of ashamed, then I can see things more clearly and make better decisions for myself.

W. D.:   Exactly.

STEP 9   IDENTIFY AND ASSESS ANY META-EMOTIONAL PROBLEMS IF RELEVANT

From her question at the end of Step 7, it seemed that Karen was ready to move towards considering how she could change her feelings of shame to those of disappointment. Thus I did not at this point assess the presence of a meta-emotional problem. I did so later on and found that Karen did not have a meta-emotional problem about her shame or social avoidance.

STEP 10   TEACH THE B–C CONNECTION

In the process of teaching the B–C connection, I used an example unrelated to Karen's own problem. By doing so, I hoped to help her understand with greater objectivity the distinction between rational and irrational beliefs.

W. D.:   The first step to changing your feelings from shame to disappointment is to understand what determines your feelings. Now, would a hundred women of your age all feel ashamed if their friends looked down on them?

Karen: No, I guess not.

W. D.:   Why not?

Karen: Well, people react to the same situation in different ways.

W. D.:   Right, but what determines these different reactions?

Karen: I don't know.

W. D.:   Well, psychologists have done a lot of research that tends to confirm what the ancient philosopher Epictetus said—that people are disturbed not by things but by their views of things. So your views or beliefs about your friends looking down on you determine how you feel. Does that make sense?

Karen: Yes, it does.

W. D.:   So, if you want to change your feelings from shame to disappointment, what do you need to consider?

Karen: My beliefs about my friends looking down on me.

W. D.: Right, to change your feelings, you need to change your beliefs. I want first to help you to distinguish between two types of belief. One will lead to shame and other self-defeating emotions, whereas the other will lead to disappointment and other constructive emotions. Now, in order to do this, I want to digress for a moment and take you through an example in which I will distinguish between these two types of belief. Is that OK?

Karen: Fine.

W. D.: Now, I want you to imagine that you have 10 dollars in your purse and that your belief is that you prefer to have a minimum of 11 dollars at all times, but that it's not absolutely necessary for you to have 11 dollars. How will you feel about having 10 dollars when you want to have 11 dollars?

Karen: Somewhat concerned.

W. D.: But you wouldn't want to kill yourself, right?

Karen: Right.

W. D.: Now, this time imagine that you believe you absolutely *must* have a minimum of 11 dollars at all times—you must, you must, you must—and you look in your purse and find that you only have 10 dollars. Now how will you feel?

Karen: Depressed.

W. D.: Or anxious. Remember that it's the same situation but a different belief. Now imagine that you still have that same absolute belief that you must have a minimum of 11 dollars at all times, and this time you find that you have 12 dollars in your purse. Now how will you feel?

Karen: Relieved.

W. D.: Right, or pleased. But by holding that same belief that you absolutely must have a minimum of 11 dollars at all times, you think something that leads you to become anxious again. What do you think that thought would be?

Karen: That I might lose 2 dollars?

W. D.: Right, or you spend 2 dollars or get robbed. Now the point of this example is that all humans, male or female, rich or poor, black or white, now and in the future, will make themselves emotionally disturbed when they don't get what they believe they *must* get. And they will also make themselves miserable when they do get it because of their musts—because even when they have what they think they must have, they could always lose it. But when humans have nondogmatic desires and don't transform these desires into dogmatic musts, they will constructively adjust to situations when they don't get what they want or aren't able to take effective action to try to prevent something unpleasant from happening in the future.

STEP 11   ASSESS iB

Once I felt sure through feedback that Karen could distinguish between rational and irrational beliefs, I encouraged her to extrapolate to her own situation.

> W. D.: Now keep in mind this distinction between nondogmatic desires and dogmatic musts as we apply it to your own situation, OK?

> Karen: Fine.

> W. D.: Now, what do you think the must is about your friends looking down on you that leads to your shame?

> Karen: They must not look down on me?

> W. D.: Right, and what kind of person do you think you would be in your own mind if they did look down on you?

> Karen: No good.

STEP 12   CONNECT iB AND C

After teaching the B–C connection and encouraging Karen to apply it to her own situation, I next attempted to solidify the relationship between Karen's irrational beliefs and her feelings at C.

> W. D.: So, can you see that as long as you demand that your friends must not look down on you and as long as you believe that you are no good if they do, then you will be ashamed and tend to avoid social contact with them?

Karen: Yes, I can see that.

W. D.:   So, if you wish to change your feelings of shame to those of disappointment, what do you need to change first?

Karen: My beliefs.

W. D.:   And, more specifically, your beliefs that your friends must not look down on you and that you would be no good if they did.

STEP 13   QUESTION iB AND rB

The next step involved the use of the Socratic and didactic styles of questioning.

W. D.:   Right. Now let's take these beliefs one at a time, although they're really linked. I'm going to help you reconsider these beliefs. Let's take the first one, that your friends must not look down on you. There are basically three ways of challenging this belief. The first is to ask whether or not it is logical. Now, don't forget you have a desire, which is that you don't want your friends to look down on you, right?

Karen: Right.

W. D.:   But does it follow logically that because you don't want your friends to look down on you that they must not do so?

Karen: No, I guess not.

W. D.:   Why not?

Karen: Well, because wanting something not to happen doesn't mean it mustn't happen.

W. D.:   That's it. To demand that something mustn't happen just because we don't want it to happen is to believe in magic.

Karen: Which doesn't exist.

W. D.:   Right. Now let's consider the second way of challenging this belief, which is to ask whether or not it is consistent with reality. Now, if there really were a law of the universe that decreed that your friends absolutely would not look down on you, what could never happen?

Karen: They could never look down on me. Oh, I see. . . . I'm demanding that something must not happen which could of course happen.

W. D.: Right, that's a good insight. You would of course prefer it not to happen, but that doesn't mean that it must not happen, because it always could. Now let's consider the third way of challenging this belief, which is to consider its usefulness. Now, as long as you believe that your friends must not look down on you, what consequences of holding this belief are likely?

Karen: Well, from what we discussed earlier, I'm going to be anxious about it happening and ashamed if it does happen.

W. D.: And don't forget that it will also lead you to avoid social contact with your friends.

Karen: As has been happening.

W. D.: Right. So the belief is going to get you into trouble. Now, to sum up: The three ways of challenging or questioning a must involve asking, "Is it logical?"; "Is it consistent with reality?"; and "Will it give me good results?" Now we've seen that the answer to these three questions is no. But don't take my word for it—consider it for yourself. It is also important to apply these three questions to your nonabsolute preferences. First is your belief "I don't want my friends to look down on me, but there's no reason why they must not do so."

Karen: Well, it's logical, as long as I have such a desire.

W. D.: Right. Now, is it consistent with reality?

Karen: Well, it is reality that I have such a desire, so my desire exists; so, yes, it is consistent with reality.

W. D.: Right, and don't forget that such a belief allows for the possibility that your friends may look down on you, which your dogmatic must did not allow for. Finally, what are the likely emotional and behavioral consequences of your belief "I don't want my friends to look down on me, but there' s no reason why they must not do so"?

Karen: Well, as we said earlier, it would help me to feel disappointed and would encourage me to try to get my friends to change their minds about me.

W. D.:   Right. Now let's use our three questions with your second self-defeating belief: "I'm no good if my friends look down on me." First, is it logical to conclude that your whole self is no good just because your friends think badly of you?

Karen: I'm not sure I understand.

W. D.:   Well, let's assume that several of my colleagues are listening to our session today. Let's also assume that they not only think badly of my therapy skills but look down on me as a person. Do I have to agree with them and define myself as "no good"?

Karen: Oh, I see what you mean. I'm agreeing with my friends' definition of me.

W. D.:   Right. Now, if your friends really do look down on you—and remember, we're assuming that they really do—they would have to take a part of you and consider that bad. Then they would jump to the conclusion that because you had this bad part, all of you was bad. Is that good logic on their part?

Karen: No, it's not, because a part can never define the whole.

W. D.:   Right, and don't forget that you then agree with their bad logic.

Karen: Exactly.

W. D.:   You said just now that a part can never define the whole. That's a very good reason not to rate yourself at all, because *yourself* is too complex to be given a single rating.

Karen: So it's OK to rate parts of yourself but not the whole?

W. D.:   Right.

Karen: So, when I say, "I'm no good," I'm rating my whole self?

W. D.:   Right, and the alternative is to accept yourself as an unratable, fallible human being with good and bad aspects. So, if your friends really do look down on you, how can you respond in your own mind?

Karen: Let's see. . . . I can accept myself as an unratable, fallible human being, even if others disapprove of me.

W. D.:   Right, and how would you feel if you believed that?

Karen: Sad but not ashamed.

W. D.: Right. Now let's move on to the second question: If the belief "I'm no good" were consistent with reality, what would you only be able to do in life?

Karen: No good things, and that's obviously not true.

W. D.: Right. So what's the alternative?

Karen: Again, that I'm an unratable, fallible human being who is receiving disapproval, which is bad.

W. D.: But *you're* not bad just because *it* is. Now the third question: As long as you believe that you are no good when your friends look down on you, where will that belief get you?

Karen: Anxious and ashamed.

W. D.: And again, avoiding social contact. But let's also use the three questions with the rational alternative beliefs. Is it logical to conclude that if your friends disapprove of you, you are still an unratable, fallible human being?

Karen: Yes, it is. Their view of me doesn't change me unless I let it. I can see that now.

W. D.: Good. Now, is the belief that you are an unratable, fallible human being in the face of their disapproval consistent with reality?

Karen: Yes, it is. As I said before, I'm still the same, with or without their approval, although their approval would be nice.

W. D.: Right. Now, finally, the third point: If you believe that you are fallible and unratable in the face of your friends' disapproval, what emotional and behavioral consequences will result?

Karen: Again, I'd be disappointed but not ashamed, and I'd try to reason with them rather than avoid them.

STEP 14 PREPARE YOUR CLIENT TO DEEPEN CONVICTION IN RATIONAL BELIEFS

In order to help Karen achieve more than an intellectual understanding of her problem, it was necessary to make the point that changing beliefs is a difficult process requiring much practice.

W. D.:   Now, how often do you consider you will have to challenge your self-defeating beliefs before you begin to believe in their rational alternatives?

Karen: Quite often.

W. D.:   Right, and do you know why?

Karen: Because that's what you have to do to change a habit.

WD.:   Right. Imagine that when you were young, you wanted to learn to play tennis, and your next-door neighbor said that she would teach you. Unfortunately, she taught you all wrong, and, as you were keen, you continually practiced the incorrect strokes, not knowing of course that they were wrong. Years later, you found that your game was getting worse rather than better, so you decided to go to a tennis pro. She was able to diagnose the problem and showed you how to perform the strokes correctly. Now, what would you have to do to improve your tennis?

Karen: Practice the new strokes.

W. D.:   Right, but would you be comfortable performing the new strokes at first?

Karen: I guess not.

W. D.:   Why not?

Karen: Because I'd be used to performing the strokes incorrectly.

W. D.:   Right, they would feel natural. But would that natural feeling stop you from correcting a stroke when you realized that it was incorrect?

Karen: No.

W. D.:   Right, and it's the same thing with changing your beliefs. The next time you think about seeing your friends and feel like avoiding them, look for your belief "My friends must not look down on me, and I'd be no good if they did." Realize that this belief has become quite natural to you, but that if you don't go along with that natural feeling, you can identify, challenge, and change that belief. You can keep doing so until the new belief—"I don't want my friends to look down on me, but if they do, I can still accept myself as an unratable, fallible human being"—becomes more natural to you. Also, the more you act according to this new belief, the more you will gain conviction in the belief.

Karen: So I not only need to challenge the old belief in my head, I need to act on the new belief as well.

W. D.: Exactly—until you move from believing the rational belief in your head to really feeling it in your gut and until you can act spontaneously on it.

STEP 15   CHECK THE VALIDITY OF A

After the initial questioning of Karen's irrational and rational beliefs, I suggested we return to check the validity of her critical A (assessed in Step 6).

W. D.: Do you remember what you were most anxious about when you imagined mixing with your friends instead of avoiding them?

Karen: Yes, that they would look down on me and I would then feel ashamed.

W. D.: Do you think they would actually look down on you?

Karen: Well, one or two might, but most of them wouldn't do that. I can see that now.

W. D.: Even if your inference about your friends looking down on you is largely false, it is still very important for you to continue working to challenge and change your irrational belief. Do you know why?

Karen: Because I need to learn to accept myself no matter what others—friends or anybody else—may or may not think about me.

W. D.: Exactly.

STEP 16   NEGOTIATE A HOMEWORK ASSIGNMENT

Karen's ability to challenge her irrational beliefs, along with her understanding that it would be necessary to practice her alternative rational beliefs, showed that she was ready to undertake specific homework assignments.

W. D.:   Now, since changing beliefs takes a lot of work, it's important for you to put into practice between sessions what you learn in sessions. Can you see the sense of that?

Karen: That's what I expected.

W. D.:   Good. Now, does it make sense to apply the three questions "Is it logical?"; "Is it consistent with reality?"; and "What results will it bring me?" to your self-defeating belief: "My friends must not look down on me, and I 'm no good if they do"? And then to apply these three questions to your more constructive alternative belief: "I don't want my friends to look down on me, but there's no reason why they must not. If they do, I can still accept myself as an unratable, fallible human being"?

Karen: Yes, I'd like to review those points.

W. D.:   How often would you like to do it?

Karen: How about three times a day?

W. D.:   When and where will you do it?

Karen: Just before breakfast, lunch, and dinner, wherever I happen to be eating.

W. D.:   Fine. Now, can you see any obstacles to doing this?

Karen: No. I'm sure I can do that.

W. D.:   Good. Here is a written list of the questions to use on these occasions.

STEP 17   CHECK HOMEWORK ASSIGNMENTS

At the beginning of the next session, Karen revealed that she had been able to review the three questions as agreed upon and that she found the results helpful.

W. D.:   How did you get on with the homework assignment?

Karen: Very well. I used the three questions and can see more clearly now why the musts are self-defeating and the preferences more healthy. Also, the self-acceptance idea makes a lot of sense to me, and I've been using this idea with some of my other problems.

STEP 18   FACILITATE THE WORKING-THROUGH PROCESS

Karen was soon ready to use behavioral assignments to overcome her feelings of shame about "being dumped." She very quickly sought out her friends and told them about the breakup of her relationship with her fiancé, having practiced rational emotive imagery first. Here she vividly imagined her friends looking down on her and began to feel ashamed, then changed this feeling to disappointment while still keeping in mind her friends' negative view of her. The imagery helped her to practice changing her irrational belief to its more rational alternative. When she actually told her friends about the breakup, she was delighted to discover that they were in fact very supportive.

Karen also worked through her shame in other situations, such as work. She had previously been reluctant to ask for help whenever she could not solve a work problem. However, as she became able to dispel her shame-creating idea "My supervisor must not think badly of me, and I'd be inferior if he does," she became more willing to disclose her ignorance and ask for help. Once again, Karen was glad to learn that her supervisor was actually pleased with her new attitude of "openness," as he called it.

Karen did not have a problem with low frustration tolerance and thus reported little difficulty in carrying out her homework assignments. Most of your clients will have more difficulty than Karen in putting into practice what they learn in therapy. We suggest that you consult Ellis (2002) for a lengthy discussion of how to overcome client (and therapist) resistance.

EPILOGUE

We have now come to the end of our discussion. If you wish to develop your skills as a rational emotive behavior therapist, then use REBT with your clients, obtain expert supervision of your work, attend advanced REBT training practica, and consult frequently the more advanced texts mentioned throughout this primer. We hope that you have found this basic introduction to REBT instructive and wish you well in your future career as a rational emotive behavior therapist. Good luck!

SPECIAL FEATURES OF RATIONAL EMOTIVE BEHAVIOR THERAPY

Albert Ellis

Rational emotive behavior therapy (REBT) has several special features that distinguish it from the cognitive therapies of Aaron Beck, Maxie Maultsby, Donald Meichenbaum, George Kelly, and other proponents of cognitive-behavior therapy, as well as from other forms of psychotherapy. Some of the special features of REBT that are to be noted by REBT practitioners, especially when qualifying for one of the training certificates in REBT, can be observed in the areas discussed in the following pages.

SOURCES OF PSYCHOLOGICAL DISTURBANCE

REBT holds that what we usually call *emotional disturbance* has important cognitive, emotive, and behavioral sources and does not purely arise from, although it is heavily influenced by, thinking. It holds that "pure" thought, "pure" emotion, and "pure" behavior virtually never exist, but are usually interactional, each including important elements of the other two. REBT notably stresses *cognitive mediation,* or irrational beliefs that usually follow activating events (A's) in people's environments and that lead to emotional consequences (C's) or feelings of disturbance. But it also contends that people bring their goals, desires, and beliefs (B's) to A, and that they often make new A's out of their feelings (as when they make themselves anxious about their anxiety). Similarly, their beliefs (B's) are differentially held under certain activating conditions (A's), and their emotional and behavioral consequences (C's) have to take place in some kind of environment (A's) and along with certain kinds of beliefs (B's). REBT, then, sees virtually all thoughts, feelings, and behaviors as interactional, not monolithic; it also sees the A's, B's, and C's of REBT—people's environments, their philosophies, and their feelings and actions—as interactional and interrelated, and practically never as thoroughly independent of one another (Ellis, 1994, 1999, 2000a, 2000b).

REBT holds that people's proneness to disturb themselves, or to react self-defeatingly to external events and internal thoughts and feelings, is both innate and acquired. People are biologically prone to think and act against their own and their society's interests, but they also partially learn to do so as a result of their social upbringing. They can easily invent irrational beliefs on their own, but they also pick them up from their parents and culture. Most of the time, they probably exacerbate their natural biological tendencies to think crookedly and behave self-sabotagingly by (often unduly) heeding environmental influences. However, people are also born with tendencies to actualize themselves: to change, to use their reasoning powers, and to push themselves to overcome environmental and self-created difficulties. Once again, they also learn such self-actualizing behaviors from their parents and teachers (Ellis, 1994, 2000a, 2000b).

Perhaps more than other forms of psychotherapy, REBT emphasizes the innate tendency of people to think crookedly and engage in self-destruction and holds that this biological tendency is one of the main reasons that people frequently resist change even when they presumably want to effect it. But REBT also emphasizes the innate tendency of humans to be able to choose their disturbed thoughts, feelings, and actions—and to be able to choose to change them (Ellis, 1976, 2000b).

In addition, REBT stresses the tendency of almost all humans to create secondary as well as primary symptoms of emotional disturbance. Thus, when people make themselves seriously anxious, they frequently construct irrational beliefs about their anxiety and make themselves anxious or self-downing about that. When they are depressed, they frequently depress themselves about their depression. Although their primary disturbances often have profound emotional, behavioral, and cognitive sources, their secondary disturbances are perhaps even more cognitive because clients *observe* their primary disturbed feelings, *think* negatively about them, and *conclude* awfulizingly about their presence and continuance (Ellis, 1998, 1999; Ellis & Dryden, 1997; Ellis & Harper, 1997; Ellis & MacLaren, 1998).

ASSESSMENT OF DISTURBANCES

REBT tends to employ at times all the assessment procedures used by other cognitive-behavior therapies, but it can also be done with a minimum of these procedures in some instances. This is largely because REBT favors REBT itself as an important means of assessment and holds that, in many (but not all) cases, zeroing in on some of the client's irrational beliefs can be highly diagnostic and can particularly indicate how and under what conditions the client is likely to react to psychotherapy. For example, clients who have great difficulty in acknowledging their irrational beliefs, in recognizing that such beliefs contribute significantly to their disturbances, and in forcefully and persistently disputing them (as they are shown to do in REBT) will usually be different from other clients. Their problems in reacting to REBT will produce salient diagnostic and prognostic information

REBT notably distinguishes between healthy and unhealthy feelings when people react to some unfortunate set of events and tends to define feelings such as sorrow, regret, frustration, and annoyance as healthy, and feelings such as anxiety, depression, hostility, self-downing, and self-pity as unhealthy. REBT practitioners therefore actively look for healthy and unhealthy feelings and may at times show clients that it is appropriate to be mournful or concerned rather than depressed or horrified—and therefore, in REBT terms, they really do not have a serious emotional problem. Conversely, an REBT practitioner may refuse to try to help clients become unconcerned about, say, holding a job or the state of their physical health because lack of concern may be considered unhealthy and harmful rather than healthy and useful.

LOOKING FOR IRRATIONAL BELIEFS

Although virtually all systems of cognitive and cognitive-behavior therapy help clients look for irrational beliefs, self-defeating ideas, or dysfunctional cognitions, REBT takes a somewhat unique stand in this respect:

1. REBT holds that many kinds of evaluative irrationalities—including unrealistic, antiempirical, and illogical evaluating about adversities—tend to produce poor results for individuals and social groups. Thus people who come to psychotherapy and who are seen as being "emotionally disturbed" do not merely have *some* irrational beliefs but also almost invariably have *certain kinds* of highly prevalent irrationalities. According to REBT, the main kinds of evaluative irrational beliefs that lead to disturbance are absolutistic and unconditional shoulds, oughts, musts, demands, commands, and expectations. More specifically, almost all people who are diagnosed as neurotic (and especially as personality disordered) absolutistically and dogmatically command that they themselves *must* do well and be approved by significant others, that others *have to* treat them considerately and fairly, and that conditions of living have *got to* be reasonably easy and enjoyable.

2. If, REBT hypothesizes, people stayed rigorously with preferences, wishes, and desires, including strong ones, and did not resort to absolutistic shoulds and musts, they would rarely become neurotic. REBT therefore invariably looks for, and helps clients look for, their evaluative irrational ideas, not merely their nonevaluative overgeneralities and unrealistic notions. Thus it is highly irrational to say, descriptively and nonevaluatively, "The earth is flat," and one will probably get into some kind of difficulty if one holds this idea. But one will not tend to be emotionally disturbed unless one adds something like "The earth is flat—as it *must* be" or "I *can't stand* the earth's being round—and therefore it isn't." REBT does not contend that people cannot be disturbed without their subscribing to absolutistic evaluations instead of staying with their relativistic preferences, but it looks for and virtually always finds such unconditional evaluations when people are seriously anxious, depressed, hating, or self-downing.

3. Feelings of emotional disturbance also result from irrational beliefs other than absolutistic evaluations (i.e., from awfulizing, I-can't-stand-it-itis, and damnation of oneself and others). But these kinds of irrational beliefs seem, in most cases, to accompany explicit or implicit absolutistic musts and would rarely exist without them. Thus, when I irrationally hold, "The earth must be flat!" I then tend to conclude logically, if erroneously, that (a) "It is *awful* if the earth is not as flat as it must

be!" (b) "I *can't stand it* when the earth is not as flat as it has to be!" and (c) "I'm *no good* if I don't see the earth as being as flat as it must be!"

4. In addition to absolutistic or "musturbatory" thinking, people often contribute to their disturbances with antiempirical or unrealistic inferences. For example, they tell themselves, "Because I failed a few times, I will always fail." They personalize, overgeneralize, resort to non sequiturs, and use always-and-never thinking about their strong desires. But they especially do so when they escalate their desires into absolutistic demands and musts. Irrational, unrealistic, and illogical inference is itself an important aspect of human behavior and results in many poor outcomes. But unless it is tied to absolutistic musts and commands and to human evaluations, it does not usually result in what we call emotional disturbance.

DISPUTING IRRATIONAL BELIEFS

REBT emphasizes the use of scientific method and of logico-empirical disputing to help people change the irrational beliefs that lead them to disturbance. It often actively questions and challenges all kinds and levels of irrational beliefs, but it particularly challenges dogmatic musts and necessities and helps people change them into desires and preferences. It favors science and the scientific method in several ways that other kinds of therapy do not favor or mention:

1. It holds that people who consistently employ scientific, flexible, nondogmatic, nonabsolutistic thinking about themselves and others tend to be only minimally disturbed, and that dogma, inflexibility, and refusal to accept reality are the essence of much serious disturbance.

2. It teaches the scientific method of questioning and disputing irrational hypotheses to as many of its clients as will accept and use this method and shows them how to apply it when the therapist is not present.

3. It accepts the religious beliefs and values of its clients and shows them how to live undisturbedly with religious, mystical, or superstitious ideas. But it questions devoutness and sacredizing— whether theological, political, economic, or social—and shows people how to combat dogma and absolutism.

4. In some cases, it may use nonscientific and religious views that are antiempirical but that may help people ameliorate their disturbance and do them more good than harm (Ellis, 2000a).

THERAPEUTIC RELATIONSHIP

REBT favors the building of a good rapport with clients, uses empathic listening and reflection of feeling, and particularly uses strong encouragement to help clients look at themselves and change. At the same time, it acknowledges the dangers of building too warm or close a relationship between client and therapist. (Many clients tend to have a dire need for everyone's, including the therapist's, approval; therefore, the therapist's favoring them may help accentuate this need.)

REBT acknowledges that the therapist also may have a dire need for clients' approval and may consequently hold back from doing active disputing of the clients' irrational beliefs and from giving them onerous homework assignments. REBT therefore encourages therapists to look at their own motives for building overly warm relationships with clients. At the same time, REBT especially holds that therapists emphasize unconditional positive regard or unconditional acceptance for all clients—no matter how obnoxiously they may behave in or out of therapy. It encourages therapists to evaluate clients' acts and thoughts, but not to rate clients globally as humans, nor especially to denigrate their selves, beings, or essences in any way.

REBT often tries to show clients that they are equal and active collaborators with the therapist in looking at and changing themselves. At the same time, it sees the therapist as a highly active-directive teacher, who knows more about human personality and its disturbances than many clients and who therefore had often better take the lead in explaining, interpreting, and disputing, as well as in teaching clients to come up with better solutions to their problems.

MULTIMODAL AND COMPREHENSIVE USE OF TECHNIQUES

REBT has a distinct theory of human disturbance and how it may most efficiently be reduced. But its theory, as discussed earlier, is interactive and multimodal and sees emotions, thoughts, and behaviors as transacting and including one another. Hence, REBT has always been multimodal in its uses of many therapeutic techniques: cognitive, emotive, and behavioral. Because it emphasizes the biological as well as the social sources of human disturbance, it frequently favors the use of medication and the physical (as well as mental) techniques of psychotherapy, including diet, exercise, and relaxation techniques.

At the same time, REBT is highly selective in the methods it employs and only occasionally uses a method because it works (e.g., positive thinking). Instead, REBT looks at both the long-range and the short-range effects of employing various methods, considers many techniques more palliative than curative (e.g., cognitive distraction), and tries to emphasize those methods that lead to a profound philosophical and emotional change and that help clients *get* better as well as *feel* better (Ellis, 1999, 2000a, 2000b). It starts most clients off with those REBT methods that usually work best with certain people most of the time; if those methods fail, it goes on to the use of different methods. It doesn't compulsively choose one or several methods with virtually all clients all of the time, and it fully realizes that some clients, such as those with psychoses or mental retardation, may not be able to use some of the better methods and may have to settle for more palliative techniques (Ellis, 2000a).

Almost all forms of psychotherapy try particularly to help clients with ego problems—that is, those clients with feelings of anxiety, depression, and self-downing. REBT, although specializing in such problems, also looks for difficulties associated with low frustration tolerance (or what REBT calls *discomfort disturbance*). It assumes that most clients have both ego anxiety and some discomfort anxiety, and when one is prominent, it looks for (but does not necessarily always find) the other. It uses some of its methods to combat ego and some to combat discomfort disturbance, and it looks for the interrelationship between these two somewhat distinct, but overlapping, kinds of problems. Thus REBT shows clients how to accept themselves when they are doing poorly; it also shows them how to give up their low frustration tolerance (LFT) about working therapeutically to change themselves so that their LFT problem does not interfere with their working hard to achieve unconditional self-acceptance.

EMOTIVE ASPECTS

In keeping with its comprehensive and multimodal character, REBT almost invariably uses a number of emotive as well as cognitive and behavioral techniques. This is because its theory notes that disturbed people not only repeat, but forcefully, vigorously, and emotionally repeat, their self-defeating musturbatory convictions. Therefore, they had better use many strong, dramatic, evocative methods of changing themselves, and REBT specializes in seeing that they do so. It usually sees that clients *forcefully* dispute their irrational beliefs and that they *actively* get in touch with and work on changing their feelings. REBT practitioners, moreover, often *powerfully* show clients how they are disturbing themselves and how they will remain disturbed unless they vigorously strive for and actively commit themselves to self-change.

Toward this end, REBT usually favors a number of emotive methods, including rational emotive imagery, shame-attacking exercises, role-playing, strong self-statements, therapeutic encouragement, group support, and various other affective techniques. But, as previously mentioned, REBT employs these methods not only for their immediate benefits but also to help clients make a profound affective-philosophical change that presumably will last. At the same time, REBT tends to take a dim view of several popular emotive methods, such as the instigation and expression of hostile feelings, because it holds that these methods are likely to do more harm than good.

HUMANISTIC ASPECTS

Unlike some of the other cognitive-behavior therapies, REBT takes a definite humanistic-existential approach. It is not purely objective, scientific, or technique centered in that it adheres to the following principles:

1. It deals with disturbed *human* evaluations, emotions, and behaviors. It sees humans as the basic creators or inventors of their own emotional problems and therefore as *humanly* capable of minimizing these problems. They are innate and acquired constructivists.

2. It is highly rational and scientific but uses rationality and science in the service of humans in an attempt to enable them to live and be happy. It is hedonistic but espouses long-range instead of short-range hedonism so that people may achieve the pleasure of the moment and the future and arrive at maximum freedom and discipline.

3. It assumes that no humans, whatever their antisocial or obnoxious behavior, are damnable or subhuman. It respects and accepts all people just because they are alive and human.

4. It often helps people to maximize their individuality, freedom, self-interest, and self-control rather than to submit to the control

and direction of others (including their therapists). At the same time, it tries to help people live in an involved, committed, and selectively loving manner with other humans and to foster social as well as individual interest.

5. It particularly emphasizes the importance of will and choice in human affairs, even though it acknowledges that some human behavior is partially determined by biological predispositions and by social learning.

VIEW OF UNCONDITIONAL SELF-ACCEPTANCE

Two of the main goals of REBT are to help clients achieve unconditional self-acceptance (USA) and unconditional other acceptance (UOA) and to see that these are interrelated. If clients will fully accept themselves, they will also tend to fully accept all other humans, and vice versa. They will then enhance their individualistic self-direction and their social interest and interpersonal relationships. Rogers (1961) gave his clients unconditional positive regard and hoped that they would then model it for themselves. REBT practitioners go out of their way to give it but also actively teach their clients how to achieve it personally and interpersonally. Self-acceptance and other acceptance then become reciprocal (Ellis, 1994, 1996, 1998, 1999, 2000a).

Following Adler (1964), Korzybski (1933/1990), Tillich (1953), Rogers (1961), and other constructivist thinkers, REBT teaches clients that they can *choose* to fully accept themselves in spite of their all-too-human deficiencies and failings. It holds that serious self-denigration underlies much emotional disturbance and tries to have clients substitute, for self-damning, USA—along with, as mentioned above, UOA. It promotes both these forms of acceptance quite vigorously and persistently in several important ways:

1. Because most people automatically and unconsciously rate themselves, as well as their acts, and often feel that they must continue to do this, REBT teaches these individuals that their self-rating had better depend solely on their aliveness and humanity. That is, people can rate themselves "good," if they insist on rating themselves at all, just because they are alive, human, and unique.

2. REBT shows people that no matter what criteria they rate themselves by—whether it be external (e.g., success or accomplishment), internal (e.g., character or emotional stability), or supernatural (e.g., acceptance by God)—they really *choose* these

criteria. Therefore, they can existentially accept themselves merely because they choose to do so and require no other external criteria whatever.

3. As noted, REBT encourages people to refuse to rate their selves, totality, beings, or essences at all—to rate only their acts, deeds, and performances. By eliminating all kinds of self-ratings and merely rating acts "good" when they are self-helping and "bad" when they are self-defeating, people can most elegantly solve the problem of rating—or not rating—themselves.

4. Strong refusal to rate oneself or one's being at all can be achieved by people's merely holding the following beliefs: (a) "I am alive"; (b) "I would like to continue to remain alive"; (c) "I would prefer to be happily instead of unhappily alive"; (d) "I can do a number of things that will help me survive happily and a number of things that will not help me, so I shall label the first set 'good' and the second set 'bad' or 'unfortunate'"; and (e) "Beyond this, I don't have to go; I shall thereby try to unconditionally accept myself and enjoy myself—but not try to prove myself" (Ellis, 1962, 1991, 1994, 1996, 2000a; Ellis & Harper, 1997; Hauck, 1991).

VIEW OF EFFICIENCY AND ELEGANCE IN PSYCHOTHERAPY

REBT, unlike some other types of psychotherapy, especially strives for efficiency and elegance in therapy. To this end, it holds the following:

1. REBT aims not merely for symptom removal but also for a profound change in the basic philosophy that largely creates people's symptoms—and that usually also contributes to some other, less highlighted symptoms.

2. REBT tries to alleviate or remove most disturbances permanently, not transiently, though it acknowledges that people have a tendency, from time to time, to retrogress and reinstitute their symptoms once they have originally minimized or eliminated them.

3. REBT tries to help as many of its clients as feasible make profound philosophical changes that will deter them from creating new disturbances in the future.

4. REBT shows clients how they can quickly see what they do to create new symptoms or re-create old ones and how they can promptly

alleviate these disturbances. It motivates people to remove their symptoms as quickly as is feasible and to block their reoccurrence. Once such symptoms do reoccur, REBT encourages clients to understand how they re-created them and to work at alleviating them by using previously useful methods as well as newly created ones.

5. REBT tries to develop methods of elegant psychotherapy that require relatively little therapeutic time and effort and that produce maximum results quickly and efficiently.

6. REBT tries to develop and promote psychoeducational methods that can help clients help themselves and that also can be applied to large numbers of people rather than only to individual clients. It specializes in bibliotherapy, audiotherapy, videotherapy, talks, workshops, courses, and other media presentations in which some of the main REBT teachings can be used effectively with large groups of individuals. In this way it tries to be prophylactic as well as curative.

BEHAVIORAL METHODS

REBT almost always uses behavioral techniques of therapy, but it particularly favors in vivo desensitization rather than purely imaginative forms of systematic desensitization, especially with difficult clients who resist other methods. More specifically:

1. It holds that people rarely change their disturbance-creating philosophies unless they strongly and steadily *act* against them.

2. It frequently urges clients to make themselves deliberately uncomfortable (e.g., in performing exercise or sports) until they finally become comfortable and, perhaps, experience enjoyment.

3. It often encourages people to act against their disturbances implosively (e.g., flooding) rather than gradually, because that kind of quickly repeated action will sometimes prove to be most helpful.

REBT uses behavioral reinforcement procedures in many instances but often uses them differently than do other schools of cognitive-behavior therapy:

1. It is wary of using love or approval as a reinforcer because many people may thereby become more suggestible and less autonomous and scientific.

2. It tries to help people think through for themselves and decide on their own goals and purposes—and hence to become less suggestible and reinforceable by external influences.

3. It endeavors to help people do things (e.g., art and science) for the intrinsic enjoyment of doing them and not merely for the extrinsic rewards of, say, money or fame.

4. It encourages clients who are not easily reinforceable to use, instead of or in addition to rewards, stiff penalties when they want to change dysfunctional behaviors. But it tries to make very clear that penalties are not to be used as punishment and do not include any ideas of undeservingness or damnation.

MULTIPLICITY OF COGNITIVE METHODS

Although REBT favors disputing, skepticism, and the use of logical-empirical methods of science in helping people to see and to surrender their basic irrational beliefs, it also employs many other cognitive methods of therapy to help people change their self-defeating thinking, emoting, and behaving:

1. It often uses positive self-statements or rational beliefs and helps clients to write these down, think about them, and steadily and strongly repeat them to themselves. For example, if a client irrationally believed, "I must be loved by so-and-so in order to accept myself," an REBT practitioner would (a) illustrate how to actively dispute this idea; (b) ask, "What alternate rational statements could you make to yourself instead of this irrational statement?"; and (c) have the client write down a list of rational coping statements (e.g., "I do not need what I want" or "It is highly desirable to be loved by so-and-so, but I can also live happily without that love") and keep going over these statements every day until the client actually tended to believe them.

2. It uses many forms of cognitive distraction (e.g., relaxation methods, yoga, meditation, reading, creative writing, socializing) to help clients temporarily give up their obsessions with self-defeating ideas and actions.

3. It often uses a good deal of philosophical discussion, including existential dialogues, with clients.

4. It teaches people how to do problem solving—including how to go back to adversities (A's) and improve them.

5. It uses semantic approaches to show people how to stop using overgeneralized language such as "I *always* fail" or "Good things *never* happen to me."

6. It uses imaging techniques, including positive imagery (in which people are able to imagine themselves succeeding rather than failing at an important task) and negative imagery (as in rational emotive imagery, in which clients imagine some of the worst things that could happen to them and make themselves appropriately sorry and regretful instead of inappropriately panicked).

7. It employs modeling methods, through which clients are shown how to help themselves and how to do REBT by observing others successfully doing so.

In employing these cognitive methods, as well as in using REBT's emotive and behavioral techniques, REBT practitioners are rarely satisfied with symptom improvement—even when this improvement is radical and startling. Their main goal with most clients most of the time is to try to help these individuals achieve a profound attitudinal or philosophical change—to internalize a new way of looking at themselves, at others, and at the world. Once practitioners achieve this goal, their clients seldom seriously disturb themselves about anything that may happen to them; when they do, they immediately acknowledge their own contribution to this disturbance and get themselves to work at undisturbing themselves. Therefore, REBT is not only a theory and practice of psychotherapy but also a philosophy that holds that human disturbance is largely, although not completely, self-created, and that most people are capable of uncreating their own disturbances and of stubbornly refusing to upset themselves severely about almost anything for the rest of their lives. Although it acknowledges that most clients will only partially accept and internalize this elegant attitude, REBT strives to help as many as possible to do so.

REFERENCES
AND
RECOMMENDED
READING

Adler, A. (1964). *Social interest: A challenge to mankind.* New York: Capricorn.

Bard, J. A. (1980). *Rational-emotive therapy in practice.* Champaign, IL: Research Press.

Beck, A. T. (1976). *Cognitive therapy and the emotional disorders.* New York: International Universities Press.

†Bernard, M. E., & Joyce, M. R. (1984). *Rational-emotive therapy with children and adolescents.* New York: Wiley-Interscience.

Crawford, T., & Ellis, A. (1989). A dictionary of rational-emotive feelings and behaviors. *Journal of Rational-Emotive and Cognitive-Behavior Therapy, 7,* 3–27.

Dryden, W. (1986). Language and meaning in RET. *Journal of Rational-Emotive Therapy, 4,* 131–142.

*Dryden, W., Neenan, M., & Yankura, J. (1999). *Counselling individuals: A rational emotive behavioural handbook.* London: Whurr.

---

*Resources recommended for use with general populations.
†Resources recommended for use with specific client populations.

Ellis, A. (1962). *Reason and emotion in psychotherapy.* Secaucus, NJ: Citadel.

Ellis, A. (1976). The biological basis of human irrationality. *Journal of Individual Psychology, 32,* 145–168.

Ellis, A. (1984a). The essence of RET—1984. *Journal of Rational-Emotive Therapy, 2,* 19–25.

Ellis, A. (1984b). *How to maintain and enhance your rational-emotive therapy gains.* New York: Albert Ellis Institute.

Ellis, A. (1985). Expanding the ABC's of rational-emotive therapy. In M. J. Mahoney & A. Freeman (Eds.), *Cognition and psychotherapy* (pp. 313–323). New York: Plenum.

Ellis, A. (2002). *Overcoming resistance: A Rational Emotive Behavior Therapy Integrated Approach* (2nd ed.). New York: Springer.

*Ellis, A. (1988). *How to stubbornly refuse to make yourself miserable about anything—Yes, anything!* Secaucus, NJ: Lyle Stuart.

Ellis, A. (1991). *Psychotherapy and the value of a human being* (Rev. ed.). New York: Albert Ellis Institute.

Ellis, A. (1994). *Reason and emotion in psychotherapy* (Rev. ed.). Secaucus, NJ: Carol.

Ellis, A. (1996). *REBT diminishes much of the human ego* (Rev. ed.). New York: Albert Ellis Institute.

Ellis, A. (1998). *How to control your anxiety before it controls you.* Secaucus, NJ: Carol.

Ellis, A. (1999). *How to make yourself happy and remarkably less disturbable.* San Luis Obispo, CA: Impact.

Ellis, A. (2000a). *Feeling better, getting better, staying better.* San Luis Obispo, CA: Impact.

Ellis, A. (2000b). *Profound therapy: Helping clients to get better rather than merely feel better.* Paper presented at The Evolution of Psychotherapy Conference, Anaheim, CA.

*Ellis, A., & Dryden, W. (1997). *The practice of rational emotive behavior therapy* (2nd ed.). New York: Springer.

*Ellis, A., & Grieger, R. (Eds.). (1977). *Handbook of rational-emotive therapy* (Vol. 1). New York: Springer.

*Ellis, A., & Grieger, R. (Eds.). (1986). *Handbook of rational-emotive therapy* (Vol. 2). New York: Springer.

Ellis, A., & Harper, R. A. (1997). *A guide to rational living* (Rev. ed.). North Hollywood, CA: Melvin Powers.

Ellis, A., & MacLaren, C. (1998). *Rational emotive behavior therapy: A therapist's guide.* San Luis Obispo, CA: Impact.

†Ellis, A., McInerney, J. F., DiGiuseppe, R., & Yeager, R. J. (1988). *Rational-emotive therapy with alcoholics and substance abusers.* New York: Pergamon.

†Ellis, A., Sichel, J., Yeager, R. J., Dimattia, D., & DiGiuseppe, R. (1989). *Rational-emotive couples therapy.* New York: Pergamon.

Gendlin, E. T. (1978). *Focusing.* New York: Everest.

*Grieger, R. M., & Boyd, J. (1980). *Rational-emotive therapy: A skills-based approach.* New York: Van Nostrand Reinhold.

*Hauck, P. A. (1980). *Brief counseling with RET.* Philadelphia: Westminster.

Hauck, P. A. (1991). *Overcoming the rating game: Beyond self-love—beyond self-esteem.* Louisville, KY: Westminster/John Knox.

†Huber, C. H., & Baruth, L. G. (1989). *Rational-emotive family therapy: A systems perspective.* New York: Springer.

Korzybski, A. (1990). *Science and sanity.* Concord, CA: International Society of General Semantics. (Original work published 1933)

Maultsby, M. C., Jr., & Ellis, A. (1974). *Techniques for using rational-emotive imagery.* New York: Albert Ellis Institute.

Neenan, M., & Dryden, W. (1999). *Rational emotive behaviour therapy: Advances in theory and practice.* London: Whurr.

Passons, W. R. (1975). *Gestalt approaches in counseling.* New York: Holt, Rinehart & Winston.

Rogers, C. R. (1961). *On becoming a person.* Boston: Houghton Mifflin.

Tillich, P. (1953). *The courage to be.* Cambridge: Harvard University Press.

Trexler, L. D. (1976). Frustration is a fact, not a feeling. *Rational Living, 11*(2), 19–22.

*Walen, S. R., DiGiuseppe, R., & Dryden, W. (1992). *A practitioner's guide to rational-emotive therapy* (2nd ed.). New York: Oxford University Press.

About the Authors

Windy Dryden is professor of counselling at Goldsmiths College, University of London, and is a Fellow of the British Psychological Society and of the British Association for Counselling and Psychotherapy. He has authored or edited more than 130 books, including *Reason to Change: A Rational Emotive Behaviour Therapy (REBT) Workbook* (Brunner-Routledge). In addition, he edits 13 book series in the area of counseling and psychotherapy, including the *Brief Therapy and Counselling* series (Wiley) and *Developing Counselling* (Sage). His major interests are in rational emotive behavior therapy; eclecticism and integration in psychotherapy; and writing short, accessible self-help books for the general public.

After earning a B.S. degree from Villanova University, *Raymond DiGiuseppe* received his Ph.D. from Hofstra University in 1975. He completed a postdoctoral fellowship at the Albert Ellis Institute in 1977. Ray joined the faculty of St. John's University in 1987, where he developed a doctoral program in school psychology and received the university's Faculty Achievement Medal. He currently is professor of psychology and chair of the psychology department at St. John's. Since

1980, Ray has served as director of professional education at the Albert Ellis Institute. He has trained hundreds of therapists in cognitive-behavior therapy (CBT). He received the Jack Krasner Early Career Contribution Award from the American Psychological Association's (APA's) Division of Psychotherapy and was elected a Fellow of the APA's divisions of psychotherapy and clinical, school, and family psychology. Ray has had a history of service since joining the Association for Advancement of Behavior Therapy (AABT) in 1976 and has missed only one convention. He helped develop the Diplomat in Behavioral Psychology (1986–1987) and served on the Diplomat Board. He was associate program chair of AABT's 1995 convention and program chair (1996) of AABT's largest convention. He has served on the editorial board of AABT's journal *Cognitive and Behavioral Practice* since its founding. As convention coordinator (1997–2000) and associate convener of the World Congress (2001), Ray developed and promoted popular convention formats such as the Master Clinician series and the World Rounds demonstrations. He was elected representative-at-large in 2001. Ray has contributed to the scientific and clinical literature with five books, more than 70 chapters and articles, and more than a hundred conference presentations. His current scholarship focuses on clinical aspects of anger, on which he lectures widely. He lives with his wife and four children, ages 4 through 19, coaches the children's soccer teams, and cooks great risotto.

Michael Neenan is associate director of the Center for Stress Management in London, England. He has coauthored eight books on REBT, as well as more than 25 articles and chapters. He coedits the *Rational Emotive Behaviour Therapist,* which is the journal of the Association for Rational Emotive Behaviour Therapists (United Kingdom).